Living
With
Art

Living With Art

HOLLY SOLOMON &
ALEXANDRA ANDERSON

Principal Photographer, John Hall

RIZZOLI
NEW YORK

First published in the United States of America in 1988 by
RIZZOLI INTERNATIONAL PUBLICATIONS, INC.
597 Fifth Avenue, New York, NY 10017

Library of Congress Cataloging-in-Publication Data
Anderson, Alexandra.
    Living with art / Alexandra Anderson and Holly Solomon ;
  photographs by John Hall and others.
      p.   cm.
    ISBN 0-8478-0960-9
    1. Art—Collectors and collecting.   2. Art in interior decoration.
  I. Solomon, Holly.   II. Title.
    N5200.A46   1988
707'.5—dc19   88-5980

Editorial Director: Donald Hutter, Donald Hutter Associates
Designer: Arnold Skolnick
Production Coordinator: Marion Wheeler, Chameleon Books
Production Services: George C. Dick, Four Colour Imports, Ltd.
Set in type by David E. Seham Associates, Inc.
Printed and bound in Hong Kong

This book is dedicated to
all those who have taught us how to see

FOREWORD
9

INTRODUCTION
A Historical Perspective
12

pg. 33

Part One
Practicalities & Options

1   OF TASTE AND COLLECTING
22

2   PERSONAL ECLECTICISM
25

3   PERIOD COLLECTIŃG
28

4   COLLECTING REGIONAL ART AND REGIONAL OBJECTS
31

5   ARTIFACTS AND ART
34

6   FURNITURE AS FORM AND ART
38

7   SITE-SPECIFIC ART AND DECOR
42

8   INSTALLING AND ARRANGING ART
46

9   SPATIAL AWARENESS
54

10   OTHER ROOMS AND SPECIAL AREAS
58

11   MASTERPIECES
64

12   LIGHTING
68

13   ISSUES OF FRAMING
73

14   USING PROFESSIONALS
78

pg. 45

Part Two
Environments

15   A MARRIAGE OF ART AND DESIGN
82

16   AN INGENIOUS APPROACH
89

17   A UNIFYING EYE
93

18   COLLECTING FOR THE FUTURE
98

19   AN ADVENTUROUS COLLECTION
106

20   UNTRADITIONAL ELEGANCE
110

21   DISCOVERING A CULTURE
116

22   A TWENTIETH CENTURY CLASSIC
121

23   "YOU LEARN FROM LIVING WITH THE ART"
124

24   TRANSFORMING THE MUNDANE
130

25   A LIFELONG EDUCATION OF THE SENSES
135

26   A FLAIR FOR REFINEMENT
142

27   VISUAL POWER
146

28   CONTEMPORARY ART IN HAWAII, FOLK ART IN VERMONT
153

29   AN ATTRACTION TO THE PAINTERLY
160

30   A JOURNEY OF DISCOVERY
165

31   EXTRAVAGANTLY PERSONAL
172

32   A COLLECTOR OF THE MOMENT
177

33   A SENSE OF MONUMENTAL FORM
183

34   A SPIRITUAL VIEW
190

35   TRACKING THE IMAGINATION OF A GREAT ARTIST
195

AFTERWORD
by Holly Solomon
202

APPENDIX
Acquiring Art / Conservation Considerations / Art Insurance,
Collection Documentation, and Other Security Matters / A Directory of
Recommended Art Services and Sources
210

PHOTO CREDITS
216

pg. 92

FOREWORD

All too frequently we hear people who are interested in collecting art express uncertainty about what to do with it in their homes—whether or not a certain painting will "fit over the couch," or if the blue and orange abstraction will upset the balance of the beige color scheme of the dining room. Holly Solomon is asked such questions all the time at her gallery. It is one of the reasons we wrote this book. There are significant distinctions between art and decor . . . and much popular confusion. By and large such confusion is unnecessary *if* one is seriously willing to learn about and be guided by the art one chooses. While it's true that through much of our history art in the home has functioned as an element of decoration, serious art, with the exception of commissions, has rarely been created or collected for that purpose. In our time especially, the private collection and domestic display of art has been increasingly informed by the art itself—by its quality, resonance, and personal meaning. So there are no broad rules or quick answers for these questions we hear about how one should live with art. On the other hand, there are options and practical considerations—a wide field of opportunity and challenge for the collector's intimate involvement—and these we have tried to address and summarize, more by way of suggestion and example than by dictate, in the first part of this book.

Beyond such applications, however, true inspiration comes from inspiring examples, and so, in the second part, we offer the environments of a selective, diverse group of contemporary collectors who have achieved, each in his or her own way, notably successful expressions of art in domestic settings. Their success has not been to the exclusion of an interest in and knowledge of the decorative arts, but the overriding consideration has almost invariably been the creation of a personally satisfying home that combines art and decor—a place that somehow, often quite magically, adds up to more than the sum of its individual parts. Such environments are eloquent extensions of the individuals who have created them. They demonstrate emotional and intellectual response; they are characterized by independent and often stubborn vision. As collections, they can become the basis of museum bequests that serve to inform public opinion and preserve the art of the future.

We hope that *Living with Art* will encourage other such independent expressions. Art in your home does not require the demanding considerations of museum or gallery display. It is a changing, even day by day experience that should always leave you the freedom to make your own choices. We also hope the book serves as a practical reminder and guide to some of the responsibilities that are part of owning and displaying art, including its care and preservation.

The collectors whose environments are represented through these pages have generously shared with us their experience, accrued knowledge, and love of art. Without them this book would not have been possible, and we thank them all for their participation. We would also like to thank Donald Hutter, who initiated *Living with Art* and has been an essential partner in its completion. Nor could we have done the book without John Hall's unflagging cooperation and his exceptional photography that has captured the spirit of so many extraordinary and different collections. Our thanks go as well to Dennis Adrian, Robert Perkins, Howard Brandston, Hester Diamond, Paula Waxman, Hallie Halpern, Robert and Gillian Crozier, Dr. and Mrs. Dixon Spivy, Barbara Burn Dolensek, Steven Wagner, Richard Hare, Trevania Dudley, David Leiber, Chuck San Clemente, and Teresa Schmittroth, with special appreciation and thanks to S.O.J. Spivy for his support and copy-editing skills, and to Genevieve and Oscar Anderson and Lafcadio Cortesi. We are grateful to all for their assistance, encouragement, and advice.

Holly Solomon and Alexandra Anderson
April, 1988

INTRODUCTION:
A Historical Perspective

The impulse to collect is basic to human nature. So is the need to embellish our surroundings. The former boxing champion Reuben "Hurricane" Carter mentions the liberating effect of some reproductions of paintings by Monet and Gauguin during the almost twenty years he spent in prison, many of them in solitary confinement. The addition of those pictures, Carter says, "meant that it was no longer a cell, but a free man's home."

Anthropologists now believe that some of the earliest cave paintings may have been created with the special purpose of "recording a series of illustrated legends or traditions, for domestic decoration as well as for ritualistic and initiatory purpose." Greek sculpture and painting, Etruscan tomb frescoes, and the breathtaking illusionistic and geometrical compositions that decorated the walls of wealthy Romans' villas at Boscoreale and Herculaneum in the first century A.D. all had decorative as well as symbolic purposes.

Though the history of the development of the decoration and design of domestic interiors is a different story from that of the development of art collecting, the two narratives intersect when we examine how people through the ages have lived with art.

Until the advent of the portable easel picture, paintings installed in domestic interiors were generally incorporated into decorative schemes that combined architectural ornament, sculpture, furniture, and decor into a unified design. As decorative arts historian Charles McCorquodale makes clear in his *History of the Interior*, "Every man-made form in the ancient world with any pretentions to design 'spoke' the same language. This gave a remarkable degree of unity to the visual arts, a unity which would seem monotonous to the twentieth century's diversified expectations." Until the Renaissance, the motifs and subject matter of these decorative schemes were pervasively religious. Pagan and Christian deities in various guises appeared on everything from walls and floor mosaics to furniture, mirrors, and eating utensils.

While this iconographic unity still exists in some Asian and Southeast Asian cultures, it was shattered in the West with the spread of secularized interest in science and geography as well as the humanist studies that reintroduced Classical ideas to the Renaissance. Interest in secular subjects taken from nature began gradually to emerge—on the borders of illuminations and in tapestry backgrounds—in the Middle Ages. The Emperor Charlemagne is known to have had a table made of precious metals and engraved with a celestial map. Stylized renderings of plants and animals, portraits of church fathers and nobles, allegories of the seasons, history, or the liberal arts appeared in metalwork, stained glass windows, church sculpture, and the tapestries which were among the first portable artistic treasures.

During the Renaissance the domestic interior became one of the finest and most concerted expressions of the culture. Artists from Mantagna to Botticelli and Raphael were commissioned by popes and princes to decorate the interiors of palaces and grand apartments. They not only contributed paintings but also oversaw the entire design for the room. As worldly display and private artistic patronage increased, many more wealthy families hired artists to decorate their homes. Some even bankrupted themselves in the competitive pursuit of the finest interior decoration and art. Lorenzo di Medici, a prototypical grand collector, patronized Michelangelo and amassed well—known collections of ancient coins, cameos, and fragments of antique Greek and Roman sculpture. Rich Renaissance families were also keen patrons of their own contemporary art on a lavish scale. Most twentieth century interiors pale in comparison with resplendent Renaissance rooms like Francesco di Medici's Studiolo in the Palazzo Vecchio in Florence. This extraordinary room is completely covered with allegorical paintings by Giorgio Vasari, who also designed the intrinsic decorative scheme with its niches for sculpture, its elaborate gilded framing systems, and its elegant ceiling rosettes. Harmonious architectural proportion, based on the ideal proportions of the human body, strict symmetry, and the subjugation of details to the whole characterize such sixteenth century rooms.

It is difficult for twentieth century collectors to imagine and nearly impossible for them to duplicate the unified grandeur of these Renaissance interiors. Americans with virtually unlimited wealth tried to produce such lavish houses at the turn of the century when the Vanderbilts built their townhouses in New York and their "cottages" at Newport. There architect Richard Morris Hunt interpreted Versailles and other European palaces when he built The Breakers and Marble House on the cliffs overlooking the Atlantic with the help of hundreds of imported Italian craftsmen.

It was the seventeenth century that spawned modern ideas of furnishing and interior decoration as a combination of compatible elements and began the concept of eclectic agglomerations of furniture, art, and decor. Pattern books and travelling artists helped spread the influence of Italian art and design throughout Europe and dictated princely tastes in France and, to a lesser extent, in Germany. The Baroque Age created such memorable interiors as the state bedroom at Chatsworth in

Frescoes from Boscoreale: "Bedroom M," one of the best preserved examples of Pompeiian domestic wall decoration, as reconstructed in the Metropolitan Museum.

England, and the gallery of the Palazzo Farnese in Rome. Frescoes were illusionistic and spilled beyond their frames, as did the exuberant sculptures that ornamented ceilings and "supported" architectural elements. During the seventeenth century France established its aristocratic taste as the leading influence on the rest of Europe. Under the Sun King, Louis XIV, painter Charles Le Brun produced the great Grands Appartements de Versailles, some of which served as backdrops for the king's collections of old master paintings. These were hung in symmetrical groups on the ornately ornamented walls. It was also in the seventeenth century that the bourgeoisie began to consolidate the wealth that allowed them to become artistic and architectural patrons.

At about the same time the Dutch bourgeoisie, made rich by their country's liberation from Spanish domination and by the emergence of the Netherlands as the major world power, began to decorate their rather somber Baroque houses with the portraits and genre paintings of Jan Vermeer, Pieter de Hooch, Rembrandt, and Gerard Ter Borch. The Dutch passion for collecting paintings was not dissimilar to the art acquisitiveness of twentieth century collectors.

François Boucher, Jean Honoré Fragonard, Jean Antoine Watteau, and Jean Baptiste Chardin supplied fanciful pastorales, still-lifes and delectable romances for the interiors of the French aristocracy and nouveau-riche class, both of whom wanted more intimacy and comfort in their domestic surroundings. The development of what is now called the rococo also established the arrangement of public and private rooms that one still finds in traditionally styled European houses and apartments. However, patrons still expected their paintings to function within unified decorative schemes.

The urge and ability to collect art had begun to expand beyond the traditional confines of the nobility, the church, and the state. While these powerful classes customarily acquired (by purchase, pillage, or patronage on a lavish scale) and displayed art as evidence of their power, status, and wealth, the development of more widespread collecting, and the subsequent development of museums as public repositories of art, comprise a very recent event in the Western hemisphere. It took the impetus of the French Revolution to transform the nature of the private museum into an institution for the education of the public. Until 1800, museums were the private preserve of the aristocracy, and collections reflected the tastes of their privileged owners.

It was during the eighteenth century that the rage for the antique, fueled by the archeological excavations at Pompeii and Herculaneum, created an international neo-classical style and dictated a taste for collections of every kind of antique sculpture and fragment. While collecting activity had expanded well beyond the boundaries of royalty by the beginning of the century, and scholars had already begun to assemble varieties of "cabinets of curiosities"—collections motivated more by scientific than aesthetic interest—the first handbook in the fields of collecting and museography was not published until 1727. Collections of curiosities and antiquities like that of Sir Hans Sloane in England (whose collection was opened to the public in 1759 and became the nucleus for the British Museum) grew more common as scientific and archeological interests expanded and as the Grand Tour introduced increasing numbers of people to the remains of Greek, Roman, and other exotic cultures. This Age of Enlightenment was also characterized by a proliferation of private art galleries, attached to the grand country houses and townhouses of the wealthy.

One of the most intriguing collectors of the early nineteenth century was the British architect, Sir John Soane. Profoundly influenced by his years in Italy, Soane combined archeological, architectural, and aesthetic interests in the house he designed and built for himself in Lincoln's Inn Fields in London. Now open to the public as a museum, the house demonstrates a flamboyantly eclectic approach to both collecting and architecture. Antique sculpture and fragments used as integral ornament are combined with ingenious displays of landscape and portrait painting, and it is here that one finds the great cycle of paintings by William Hogarth, "The Rake's Progress," hung cleverly on folding walls that open to make an interior window.

Another distinguished British collector of the period, the architect Thomas Hope, issued tickets so that members of the Royal Academy could view his London house. Hope's polycultural approach to architectural and furniture design created a rich stew of cultural influences; he borrowed motifs and forms from Egyptian, Greek, Roman, Turkish, Chinese, and Indian prototypes. A collector of contemporary sculptures by John Flaxman and Antonio Canova, Hope also displayed a weakness for antique vases and sculpture. Zealous in his desire to proselytize his tastes, Hope wished to "contribute my mite not only towards remotely giving new food to the industry of the poor, but new decorum to the expenditure of the rich." Such sentiments also represent the initial stirrings of a democratization of taste that was greatly accelerated by the Industrial Revolution.

Until the twentieth century, Americans derived their ideas of domestic architecture, design, and artistic worth from European and other foreign sources. And it was in America that these ideas were most rapidly simplified and democratized. The country's first museum, established in Philadelphia by painter Charles Wilson Peale in the late-eighteenth century, was a

A bedroom of the Palazzo Sagredo, Venice, c. 1718, as reconstructed in the Metropolitan Museum.

hodge-podge of artistic, scientific, and botanical displays (including a stuffed elephant). It was a provincial cabinet of curiosities on a grand and eccentric scale that had begun as the artist's private collection.

The nineteenth century produced methods of manufacture and reproduction that vastly facilitated the production of everything from furniture to carpets, *objets d'art*, and building materials. One stylistic revival followed another in dizzying profusion. Domestic decor in Europe and America moved through Greek, Roman, Egyptian, and Renaissance revivals, embraced exoticism in the form of oriental influences, and produced the opulent clutter of high Victorianism and the utopian sensibility of the Arts and Crafts movement. The heady days of the Gilded Age in the 1880s and 1890s brought to the fore the self-conscious aestheticism of Oscar Wilde as well as a generation of American merchant princes who, with their wives,

*Marble House, Newport, built 1889–1892 by William K. Vanderbilt:
the dining room, adapted from the Salon of Hercules, Versailles, by
Richard Morris Hunt.*

Sir John Soane's house according to documentation of how it looked in his day, c. 1825: the breakfast parlor, the library from the dining room, the dome, and the south drawing room.

Above: *Installation of the living room from the Francis W. Little house, designed by Frank Lloyd Wright, in the American Wing of the Metropolitan Museum. Art and artifacts are subsidiary elements to the unified decorative scheme of Wright's Arts-and-Crafts-influenced house, built 1912–1914 in Wayzata, Minnesota.*

Opposite: *Gertrude Stein's salon in her house at 27 rue de Fleurus reflects this great American collector's disregard for decorative conventions and her discerning taste for the avant-garde art of her time.*

attempted to emulate the splendor of their European predecessors in their domestic arrangements and art collections. Other late-nineteenth century collectors were motivated by an emerging historical consciousness, particularly with the advent of the Colonial revival movement at the turn of the century, to put together the earliest collections of American art and antiques, while artists, intellectuals, and aesthetes were influenced in their tastes by an exposure to oriental art that reached its apogee at the 1886 Philadelphia Centennial Exhibition.

The stringent winds of twentieth century modernism encouraged radical changes in art and design in both Europe and America and influenced members of the upper middle class and high bohemia to take up collecting as an exercise in demonstrating one's affinity with new ideas rather than as a display of wealth and social status. Gertrude Stein's collection of modern art exemplified this understanding of art as an affiliation with radical thinking, as did many of the pioneering collections put together by other early-twentieth century American collectors who were not necessarily wealthy.

Nevertheless, art collecting at the highest level has remained a province of the rich. The huge prices for paintings, sculpture, and decorative art objects breathlessly recorded these days in newspapers and magazines and on television make it seem that objects of quality are currently beyond most people's reach. Yet the instinct to acquire, organize, and display beautiful and interesting things flourishes today. Crafts, folk art, industrial design, architectural drawings, recent artist's furniture, photography and architectural design have all joined the ranks of the collectible. Shrewd collectors continue to seek out and find the undiscovered category, the unfashionable art work, or the new talent, whether or not money is a consideration. "There's always something to collect," says artist Philip Pearlstein. "One just has to be smart." In every age collectors have reflected the ideas and tastes of their period, even as they give coherence to the prevailing styles of the day. Great collectors possess an inner vision that they consciously or unconsciously seek to fulfill in everything they buy. Shrewd and imaginative collectors revive the overlooked through their personal activities. As artists, architects, and designers—so often collectors in their own right—synthesize or borrow artistic ideas from the past, new styles are created. The nineteenth century saw an evolving series of "revival" styles, which rapidly cannibalized the past and other cultures in a way not unlike the recent nostalgic revivals where everything from the furniture of the 1950s to art deco and nineteenth century English country house decor became codified and popularized.

Collectors in the late-twentieth century continue to support these emerging artistic styles, passionately acquiring works of art in an age that seems surfeited with visual images. While television, movies, and advertising bombard us with sophisticated, endlessly replicated pictures, painting and sculpture retain their allure. The interest in design and home decoration, now democratized, has never been more widespread. Examples of great craftsmanship from every period are sought with unflagging energy. People continue to want to create environments that express their individuality, their knowledge, their taste. Beyond displays of wealth or status, collecting still offers enormous satisfactions. Lydia Winston Malbin defined one of the most convincing reasons for the activity when she observed, "When I started collecting, I never thought of the value my works would have in the future. I collected simply because I believed in the artists and their concepts. Collecting twentieth century art fulfilled an inner need. Living with art became a way of life for me and my family."

Part One
Practicalities
&
Options

1

OF TASTE
AND COLLECTING

Conceptions of taste are under continual challenge and revision. As social commentator and writer Russell Lynes points out in his book, *The Tastemakers*, "I do not know what *good* taste is. I do know that taste is not constant and that it is a creature of circumstance. . . . Furthermore it becomes apparent that not only is one generation's good taste very likely to be the next generation's bad taste, but one individual's ideas about what is good taste and bad taste change as he matures, moves to a different place or a different way of living, and acquires new sets of values for judging not only his surroundings but also what he wants out of life. . . . Good taste and bad taste, adventurous and timid taste, cannot be explained by wealth or education, breeding or background. . . . Taste is our personal pleasure, our private dilemma, and our public facade."

Archetypal notions of "good taste" often have been segregated and defined by likes and dislikes attributable to class, region, or culture, creating shifting battle zones in the process. But artists are continually breaking down notions of established taste, challenging all divisions and expanding definitions. Great art, though it may be reinterpreted by each age, exists beyond changing canons of taste.

There are those who innovate taste and those who refine it. Fashion—the embodiment of prevailing or established taste—is increasingly dictated by the media, and when it comes to art such fashionable taste becomes the most treacherous even if the most noisily pursued arbiter of quality. Fashions in art are especially perfidious since today's rage may be tomorrow's discard, and people who are swayed by such fashions in their collecting of art may not sufficiently trust their own knowledge and intuitions when they acquire works of art. The value of an artist's work cannot be judged by whether it is fashionable or unfashionable.

Artists, shrewd collectors, and seasoned art dealers repeatedly stress that each person must develop his own taste—his own vision—through what fundamentally amounts to a continuing self-education. The exercise of informed personal choice allows a collector to repeatedly challenge his own rules and in the process expand his visual understanding. Art that initially breaks those rules, that may even appear unacceptibly aggressive or "too" strange, pretty, or ugly, may offer new perceptions and radical visual ideas. It can be invigorating to find yourself breaking your own value systems about what you thought interested you when you recognize art's capacity to challenge and redefine taste. Though people are motivated to collect by every conceivable reason, one of the most compelling may be that collecting allows an individual to continually question, examine, and redefine his tastes.

There are as many underlying motives for collecting as there are collectors. Some are born collectors who accumulate and categorically arrange stamps, rocks, shells, or dolls as children. Others collect as if they were detectives, hunters, or historians. Still others are driven by psychological needs. Some collectors love the very activity of buying; some are consumed with a passion for a particular medium, artist, or period of art history; some use collecting as a demonstration of power, status, or wealth, fulfilling Thorstein Veblen's definitions of conspicuous consumption.

While there is no dependable definition of taste—good, bad, high, low—cultivating one's own taste increases one's faculties for involvement. The *effect* of taste, what taste can lead to, is what makes a difference in our lives. One keystone of taste is the capacity for *aesthetic judgement*. However an interest in art begins, the ensuing stages of personal aesthetic judgement are continuing steps in the increasing ability to make distinctions and informed choices, and to be able to have an educated appreciation of why something moves you, forces you to think, or impels you to acquire. There are endless ways to improve those abilities to discriminate. Collectors go back to school. They also learn from their travels through the on-site study and direct experience of art, architecture, design, or anthropology. They seek out experts in the fields that interest them, who can share the knowledge that leads to connoisseurship. Nothing can replace the study of the objects themselves in gaining that knowledge, a fact which the collectors represented in this book emphasize repeatedly.

Certain collectors may relish the idea of discovering artists who have yet to be recognized; judging the caliber of such emerging works is one of the most challenging areas of art collecting since few clues about the development and ultimate reputation of the work are available until a later time. People who realize that they are caught up as direct witnesses, or even as participants in a particular moment of great creativity—an artistic movement in their own era—have established collections that capture the spirit of that era. Such collectors recognize that they were "in the right place at the right time" and took advantage of the privilege.

Other collectors may tire of artistic movements once they have become widely recognized, ratified by prevailing taste, or popularized, and will then turn to a more arcane or neglected area. One British connoisseur of Color Field painting (who acquired his pictures in the mid 1960s) sold off his collection at the height of the movement's popularity, after the paintings had risen considerably in monetary value (with many becoming even more valuable by a decade later). He then turned to creating his own cabinet of curiosities in the eighteenth century manner and was able to buy artifacts from the important Pitt–Rivers collection that were being de-accessioned by the Ashmolean Museum. He also relentlessly combed every possible

source for additional prehistoric and scientific curiosities.

The exercise of taste can in itself be a form of creativity, for through challenging selection and juxtaposition of art a collector can create something unique and significant out of the galaxies of existing art and objects. The antiquities collection of Sir John Soane was a powerful statement about the classical world and the neo-classical intellectual and artistic curiosity of the eighteenth and early nineteenth centuries. Such assemblies promote changed perceptions and enlarged understanding. Great private collections become recognized as repositories of culture and

Expressions of taste: restrained but powerful minimal art combined with elegant modern furniture; spirited and brilliantly colorful contemporary American art with comfortable and casual furniture.

23

knowledge that subsequently enrich the understanding of others. In New York, both the Frick Collection and the Pierpont Morgan Library are examples of the value of the private collector's passion.

The asset of a trained "eye" is also important, whether one is collecting against or in the midst of prevailing artistic styles. While having such an eye may be partially intuitive, a great deal can be learned. The pursuit and acquisition of an ongoing education about art is a collector's prerequisite. Herbert and Ruth Schimmel (see Chapter 35) have gained a knowledge over a forty-year span about the art of Henri de Toulouse-Lautrec and his period that enables them still to find objects of the period in odd shops and unexpected, out-of-the-way places in France. The Schimmels know more about the artist than do many professional art experts.

It can also be beneficial for the collector to recognize that the art and decorative arts of one culture are often little recognized or undervalued by another culture, just as did a California collector of modern painting who also acquired Mimbres pottery before it was widely appreciated in America. Artist Nabil Nahas (Chapter 26), whose ongoing interest had been in the best of the French modern painters, was often able to acquire examples of their work much less expensively in America than they would have cost if bought in Paris.

Chicago critic, curator, writer, and collector Dennis Adrian has accurately expressed the benefits of an ongoing exposure to art in his essay, "A Brief Personal History." He writes, "As a child I was fortunate enough to be exposed to an art education; through weekend and summer classes at a museum art school, I was introduced to the habits and joys of museum going. And, while still in high school, I had a close friend whose family lived, with an easy naturalness, among a small collection of paintings, graphics, 'primitive' (Northwest Coast American Indian) art, ceramics, and sculpture. I knew, therefore, without much thinking, that the function of such things was not only to be seen in museums, but was also to be lived with, and experienced at leisure and in depth."

Keep in mind that art itself is non-utilitarian. You buy or collect art as something precious, or unique, and the rest should follow. Art should never be acquired just to fill a space nor forced to harmonize with a color scheme. That's a tyranny of decorating. Let your interests, not your self-consciousness or insecurities, lead you. As you change, so will your domestic surroundings.

Expressions of taste: maximum concentration on energetic art; anonymous folk art with grouping as the key element; a cosmopolitan interior elegantly combining seventeenth century furniture and modern art.

2
PERSONAL ECLECTICISM

These days, the word "eclectic" very often is accompanied by a derogatory shrug. When using it to describe someone else's taste, many people seem to suggest that such eclectic taste is unfocussed, scattered, undisciplined; or worse, that the individual in question has no mind of his own but is caught up successively by every fad, with his choices of what to collect dictated by a dilletante's superficiality, a lack of focus, or a weakness for the fashionable. Indeed there may be some truth to these aspersions. In the introductory notes for the recent reissue of *The Decoration of Houses* by Edith Wharton and Ogden Codman, Jr., originally published in 1902, John Barrington Bayley remarks that every era has its "specimen rooms." "Today's [late twentieth century] specimen room," he points out, "is a little museum. It has white walls and touches every cultural base: a Congo paddle, Benin, Grosz, Navajo, a Baroque drawing, Tiffany glass, mobiles, abstracts, Op, Pop, Eames, Bauhaus."

All of us have seen such interiors. They seem to signal their residents as some breed of quickly impressionable cultural tourist through many centuries and different cultures; aesthetically-minded globetrotters who have returned with a variety of souvenirs. Perhaps a decorator has provided an instant cocktail of "interesting" accessories, some expensive, brand-name designer furniture, and a few co-ordinated bits of art. The result may be a package of acceptable sophistication, but such interiors are often no more than agglomerations of received ideas of fashionable taste; they possess little depth or personal meaning.

There are endless, more rewarding varieties of the eclectic interior. And in this era, when cultural and artistic pluralism have reached a new height of self-consciousness, the mixing of periods and styles is one of the most common modes people chose when they begin furnishing their rooms, forming their collections, and embellishing their surroundings. In these kinds of domestic settings, traditional hierarchies of values and the formalized, more ritualistic patterns of living are eradicated, and such interiors at their best become maps of individual enthusiasms and gathered experience, driven by a series of interests or an attraction to diversity.

For an expression of *personal* eclecticism, it is individual

Above: *Composition of disparate art and artifacts in a carefully scaled arrangement.*

Below: *In this period group, a bronze statuette by Maude St,. Jewett is lit by designer Donald Desky's geometric lamp while a 1930s digital Kem Weber clock is reflected in a 1928 mirror by Emile-Jacques Ruhlmann.*

A contemporary painting with French chairs and a custom-designed table emphasize bold color contrasts.

Opposite above: *A combination of art and furnishings of different cultures, periods, and materials gives character to this open loft.*

Opposite below: *Contemporary art contrasts with traditional furnishings and decoration.*

choice that operates as unifying principle over the formation of interiors and collections. Think of how many living rooms, how many houses you have seen overwhelmed and confused by what is just an assortment of objects—a couple of landscape paintings, a sofa busily covered in flowered chintz, a contemporary chair, various vases and bibelots—all comfortable enough but somehow banal. There is no identifiable *person* in residence. Then think of the houses that have imprinted on them a style redolent of visual biography, of the characters of their owners.

One such place, now dismantled, was a dark, unusually dusty, high-ceilinged studio above Carnegie Hall. It belonged for many years to a worldly portrait painter who was a passionate lover of the theater. The surfaces of old, plain pine or cherry tables were scattered with small sculptures in bronze and plaster—maquettes by his sculptor friends, like Henry Varnum Poor—and photographs of actors and musicians he knew. Most of the paintings which packed the walls were either his own—large brooding portraits of Pablo Casals and Bette Davis—or pictures by artist friends no longer particularly well known. The rest were folk art portraits, bought within a hundred mile radius of his house in Maine. The glue that held this diversity together was not only his love of the human face but, more, the studio's containment of a personal record—this lifetime accretion of one man's memorabilia and personally meaningful art. The character of that room, its true *value*, came from the impassioned life of its inhabitant.

Collecting art is like a diary of your life. At least that is what it can become as an accrual of your own personally eclectic spirit. Acquiring art is an investment of time and energy, not just money, so why not do it with passion—because the art is something you *must* have. And consider too that the works you buy should become more meaningful with time. That is one way to differentiate between art and decor. If a work of art doesn't fit into a particular decor, find another place for it. Holly Solomon frequently advises people to put a piece of art away for a while, if they become unhappy with or tired of it, and look at it again at another time. A lot of collectors put art in storage if they find it hard to live with for one reason or another. The meaning of objects can change, so always exercise great caution in discarding art too quickly. As a document of your life—where your interests, heart, and mind have been, even where and how they have changed—your art remains both a record and measure of your inner worth.

3
PERIOD
COLLECTING

For at least the last thirty years, historical revivals of past styles have followed one another at a pace even more furious than the parade of historical revivals during the latter half of the nineteenth century. In this century, art nouveau was already being rehabilitated during the late 1950s and early 1960s. There quickly followed a revival of interest in art deco and art moderne, and then a rediscovery of the design of the 1950s, which reached its height by the early 1980s.

Concurrently, more historically minded collectors concentrating on pre-twentieth century periods were bringing back much of what rigorous modernist canons had regarded as anathema. These collectors and decorative arts historians refocussed on the strengths of everything from Empire furniture and the elaborate forms of the Victorian era to the four-square solidity of the Arts and Crafts movement and the eclectic cultural mix of forms of the Aesthetic Movement. Even modernism became regarded as a period style as many contemporary architects and designers abandoned the rigors of the International School for the appropriations of postmodernist pastiche.

While revivalism has been a strong current in architecture and the decorative arts, it has also been demonstrated in the recent revisionist interests of artists and art historians, who have been busy reinterpreting the reputations and ideas of past artists and other cultures.

Most collectors create a varying eclectic mixture of art, furniture, and design objects, but some become fascinated by a single historical or stylistic period. They concentrate on creating a collection that is limited—more or less faithfully—to that period. At a time when historic preservation has gained wide support, increasing numbers of people have become more aware of the value of past architectural and artistic styles. At Edgewater, a nineteenth century, Greek Revival mansion on the banks of the Hudson River, collector and preservationist Richard Jenrette has expended great effort to restore both the exterior and interior of the house to evoke its original period. Art and furniture, as well as wall colorings, rugs, and light fixtures, are examples of American art and decorative arts of the mid-nineteenth century. Mr. Jenrette also specifically wanted to have the house display a relationship to the southern roots of its original owners, and much of the art and furnishings at Edgewater reflect this desire.

The works of art in such extremely focussed collections are enhanced by the period decor in which they are set. But even these very faithful period settings have not eschewed modern conveniences, nor can they be altogether faithful reproductions of a given period. The collectors have not let their devotion to the authenticity of an historical moment overwhelm their own practical needs. They have *interpreted* rather than reproduced the past.

Even the period rooms carefully installed by museums as objects of study cannot reproduce the past with absolute authenticity. Whether it be Winterthur or the Metropolitan Museum of Art, or any of the other museums that have addressed themselves to the study of culture through decorative objects and replicated interiors, improved scientific methods of study have led to considerable revision in curatorial ideas of what is in fact authentic at any given period. Many of these period rooms have been redone several times in continuing attempts to improve their accuracy.

Objects, works of art, fabrics and paint colors have inevitably changed with time. They may have faded, become discolored, or have been extensively restored. Collectors of furniture know that the more untouched an object is, the greater its value. Yet few collectors opt for an utterly purist approach, even when they create a period setting for their acquisitions. "Such settings," says Witold Rybczynski in his recent book, *Home, A Short History of an Idea,* "are rarely meant to be historically accurate; they are intended primarily to create an appropriate mood." Collectors who wish to pursue and display the art and design of a particular historical period have to temper their devotion to authenticity with a practical regard for the realities of domestic living.

A period collection of art by Henri de Toulouse-Lautrec, art nouveau metalwork, glass, and ceramics, with furniture by Marjorelle and Gallé.

Above: *Sarah Bernhardt's house was a reflection of her legendary career, personality, and time. In this room, reconstructed for the Wildenstein Gallery, the bust of the actress, her feather fan, and several portrait drawings are arranged in a setting of oriental rugs and chinoiserie.*

Right: *Edgewater, a restored mansion on the banks of the Hudson River, is evocative of nineteenth century aristocratic tastes.*

4
COLLECTING REGIONAL ART AND REGIONAL OBJECTS

In a historical sense, virtually all art is regional. It is work inspired by artists with creative roots in a certain region who bring with them, or are profoundly influenced by, stories, affections, ideas, and rituals drawn from the life around them. The best of this work is so intelligent—whether acknowledging art history or revising it—so well crafted, inspiring, and commanding that it becomes internationally accepted as a new chapter of art history. Thus Wassily Kandinsky was one of those instrumental in moving our century into the realms of abstract art—with Russian folk art as his source of inspiration, both aesthetically and politically. This is what might be called the regional internationalism of art. Pablo Picasso was Spanish, but when he moved to Paris he already understood the Parisian art world. When you travel, you realize how Spanish Picasso is, how German Bauhaus . . . There are precedents in local tradition that artists seem to have in the blood.

Yet what we are talking about should not be confused with the genres of "regional art" that have increasingly burgeoned across the world of art collecting. There is wonderful regional art, and there is art that uses regional art as its source and inspiration. The distinction is a matter of intent. A superb Indian blanket is an artistic object in its own right, but it is still an artifact, and it is not the same as a Frank Stella work that makes affectionate use of the stripes of Indian blankets. Nevertheless, authentic regional art has its own intrinsically profound and delightful appeal, and there is no stigma of status in devoting oneself to its collection. Some of the greatest collections around the world (and in this book) make use of, even consist of, outstanding regional examples.

This world of regional art collecting, it must be said, has been irreversibly transformed by modern communications, in much the same way as have all markets of international exchange. Traders in Sumatra call Minneapolis on portable cellular telephones. Computers transmit stock market data between America, Europe, and Asia in seconds. The slick, colored photographs of glossy magazines reveal to millions the way people live, and television continues to glibly reveal the way the world looks at itself. And as collectors follow the trends, more and more collections tend to look alike—whether located in Milan, London, Los Angeles, New York, even Hong Kong—while artists themselves from different regions are increasingly

This brilliant collection offers prime examples of the raw imagery typical of paintings from the Chicago School.

Above: *Two sophisticated examples of American nineteenth and early-twentieth century found sculpture.*

Right: *American folk art objects with South American antiquities.*

Opposite, top and bottom left: *Groupings of New England farm tools, trivets, checkerboards, and rural advertising signs.*

Bottom, right: *A vibrant West African mask from Burkina Faso.*

influenced to create art that subscribes to the trends.

Still and all, strong regional differences continue to flourish in different areas and cultures, and concentrating on the specific characteristics unique to different kinds of regional art can be a richly fascinating pursuit for collectors, especially those who live at a remove from the major distribution centers of art.

Understanding the more profound cultural influences of a region becomes almost a requisite to understanding the nature of the art indigenous to that region. If one is to specialize in the artifacts of American southwest Indians, for example, a knowledge of the rituals, beliefs, and cultural history of those tribes will naturally aid the collector in making judgements about the quality of both historic and contemporary objects. In some cities—Chicago and Houston are two—strong communities of local artists have evolved distinct styles and imagery. Some of Chicago's leading collectors, like writer and curator Dennis Adrian, have concentrated on examples of regional painting and sculpture reflecting an amalgam of interests in folk art, surrealism, and realism that has compelled three generations of Chicago artists. In areas of southern California and in the state of Washington, contemporary artists and artisans have demonstrated unusual dedication to ceramics, glass, and wood as indigenous media for works representative of the communities in these areas.

Subject matter may also be regional. One collector in upstate New York concentrates on photographs and paintings that depict the Hudson River. They range from nineteenth century to contemporary works and are often by artists virtually unknown to New York galleries. Other collectors may focus on the folk arts and artifacts of their particular region. Laila and Thurston Twigg-Smith, in their Vermont farmhouse (see Chapter 28), limited their collecting to things they could find within easy traveling distance of their home.

One attraction to forming a regional collection is the adventure of inadvertent discovery. Second-hand stores, antique barns, small auctions, and artists' studios become primary sources for the regional collector. Even yard sales—which are not only great fun but also good opportunities for focusing one's vision—may yield an extraordinary find.

Regional collecting can also represent a personal record of the collector's travels, to whatever part of the world. Tom Wheelock's concentrated and unique collection of art from Burkina Faso (see Chapter 21) serves a dramatic example.

Whether your regional focus reflects a dedication to the area where you live or a fascination with an exotic and entirely different culture, collecting regional art not only offers new stores of knowledge about specific parts of a culture, it can also add an enriching element to your life with art.

5
ARTIFACTS
AND ART

Is there a categorical answer to the question "What is art?" Just as certain kinds of writing convey information but are not demonstrations of the "art" of writing, so certain man-made objects may be sociologically and culturally expressive but do not qualify as art. Out of the welter of artifacts that fill the world, few are elevated to artistic status. And the process of arbitration or decision changes with each generation. As things made by hand become increasingly scarce, they can gain in artistic status. Witness the recent ascension of certain types of ceramics, glass, textiles, and woodwork from the realms of craft to the arena of artistic appreciation.

Many categories of things that once were considered ethnographic or scientific curiosities have since been recognized as works of artistic prominence. Antiquities, pre–Columbian art, African art, and Indian baskets are today collected both as works of art and works of cultural importance.

John Stilgoe, a professor of landscape design at the Harvard School of Architecture, has observed that artifacts often become appreciated for their artistic properties after their usefulness has been superseded by other technologies. The wooden propeller, the ship's steering wheel, the weather vane, all products of antiquated technology, are now "collectibles" for their elegant forms and attractive materials. We live with them as souvenirs of an out-moded technology. Even early examples of twentieth century streamlined design—toasters, radios, irons, blenders—have become desirable for collectors who appreciate industrial design. Craftworks like the headdresses and weapons of American Indian tribes have been retrieved from cultures now extinct or close to extinction. Their aesthetic values have remained and are preserved, while their intrinsic cultural meanings may or may not be distorted.

Still, we are speaking here of artifacts, works of high craft representing certain utilitarian and sociological values, rather than works created purely as artistic expression, or works *transformed* into artistic expression. However, this differentiation between art and artifacts gets blurred when we view art itself in a strictly sociological light. Marcel Duchamp is remembered for having turned the most banal of industrial products—the porcelain urinal—into an art object when he took it out of its functional context, put it in a gallery, and called it

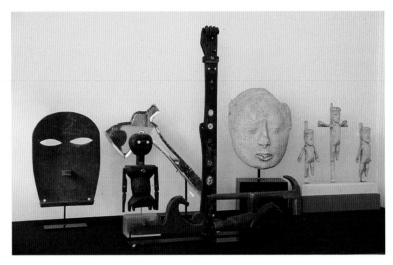

Opposite top, center, and bottom: *Part of a collection of blown glass vessels by premier American glassmaker Dale Chihuly; industrial artifacts with antiquities; a disassembled wooden sphere bearing formal affinities with a ceramic vase and a prototype of a teacup and saucer.* Above: *A modern saw painted by Jacob Cass.* Left: *A lustrous art deco ship's bar holding a twentieth century silver coffee service.*

a "readymade." Yet it should be kept in mind that when Duchamp displayed the readymade and called it art, it was the great Duchamp making that decision, challenging the authority of the artistic process of his day. Ultimately, we realize now, what Duchamp did was to challenge prevailing cultural assumptions through irony. Thus artists can function as instant transformers, incorporating the ephemeral, the lowly, or the overlooked object into an authentic work of art.

Quilts—the utilitarian productions of countless American women who took to quilting as a creative, frequently communal outlet—serve an interesting example of the interrelation possible between artifacts and art. It took the abstract, geometric compositions of constructivist, minimalist, and neo-constructivist artists to make people recognize the strong formal patterns and colors that are incorporated in the finest, most intricate quilts, products of a memorable creativity embodied in a medium—textiles—that ranks low in the hierarchies of art designated by our culture.

Turning overlooked artifacts into objects worthy of collection has become a phenomenon of our time, with categories including everything from Mickey Mouse toys to Fiestaware. Subcultural collectibles today include virtually all kinds of mass-produced memorabilia. While the categorizing, sorting, and acquiring entailed may lead to a fascinating collection, they do not necessarily transmute objects into items with intrinsic artistic worth. Such kitsch collections embody a cultural and sentimental nostalgia—enjoyable indeed, but not art.

Finely crafted artifacts can live with art. And differentiating between what is art, what is artifact, and what is artifact waiting to be recognized for its artistic meaning can be a rewarding exercise, especially for collectors of sociological, cultural, or technological sophistication.

Above: *Displays of nineteenth and twentieth century mass-produced ceramics.*

Opposite: *Weathervane animals and cast-iron toys parade across a New York apartment window.*

6
FURNITURE AS FORM AND ART

The irascible anthropologist Bernard Rudofsky declares in *Now I Lay Me Down to Eat* that "sitting on chairs is an acquired habit, like smoking, and about as wholesome." He recommends the floor as the better alternative. Certain cultures—Japanese, the Mogul Empire—shunned chairs but developed elaborate cupboards, chests, and tables. In the West, the evolution of all kinds of furniture has been raised over the centuries to a fine art. As early as the Renaissance, chairs, tables, chests, even elaborate beds were seen as an integral part of the interior decoration of a room, and by the seventeenth century, furniture in aristocratic houses had become so formal as to be almost ritualistic (Versailles serves here as a cultural model). Its shape and arrangement was strictly formal; use was secondary and ideas of comfort came last.

The strictly ceremonial and hierarchical uses of furniture do remain as vestigial remnants of the powers of church and state. But for the purposes of the collector it is most useful to consider the development of furniture of all civilizations as permutations of cultural, historical, and aesthetic expression.

Many collectors of the fine arts whose walls may glow with choice examples of painting possess furnishings as the result of undirected thought or offhand selection; or choices will have been entirely turned over to a decorator. People may opt for comfort in their surroundings, and there are wonderful art collections no less significant because the collector cares little about decor, but an awareness of decor and a knowledge of the decorative arts, especially the history of furniture design, can not only enrich the effectiveness of a collection but may prove a pleasure and reward in itself.

There are many examples of such collections in this book: of eighteenth century French furniture combined with contemporary design and modern painting; of Bauhaus furniture and American folk art; and of a suite of furniture by Jacob Des Malter paired with the designs of Jean Michel Frank and modern French painting. All of these collectors count their furniture as an extension of their collecting as well as a necessary utility.

Some collectors' interests inevitably lead them to the furniture of the period whose art is their major concern. Lautrec collector Herbert Schimmel says, "Our art nouveau furnishings are an integral part of the collection which could not have the

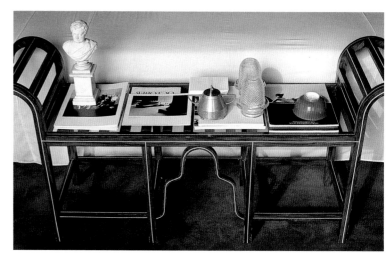

Opposite top and bottom: *A streamlined French deco chest of drawers, c. 1950, by Chevallier; pure form and line in an unusual inlaid bench.* Above left: *An elaborate multi-colored ensemble of chair, desk, and framed painting by Rodney Alan Greenblat.* Left: *Sophisticated examples of advanced twentieth century furniture and design paired with a range of contemporary art.* Above right: *Paint, fabric, and tile transform common pieces into a contemporary artist's furniture.*

same impact without them. They are crucial to the understanding of the art."

By understanding something of the history of furniture design, one can very quickly arrive at what is at least a comprehension of the formal strengths and differences in each decorative arts period. The learning process is identical to the way one learns about painting and sculpture; by reading, attending auctions, comparing objects themselves, and picking the brains of expert dealers, connoisseurs, collectors and curators. Thinking of furniture as varieties of sculptural form can help the collector to discriminate between various styles of antique and modern furniture.

Applying the ideas of sculptural form will also be helpful in planning the arrrangement of furniture in any given room. Even though modernism promoted the idea of the simplified, stripped-down room, contemporary interiors incline toward overcrowding. Questions of mass, grouping, and competing shapes need to be considered when putting furniture together in a room, as does whether the selected style of furniture will complement or contrast with the resident art works. There are no hard and fast rules, though one might want to resist clichés of decorating. The extent of one's involvement should rest on personal desire.

Collectors have lately been increasingly interested in the furniture designed by architects and artists. While architects have been among the foremost designers of furniture, in this as well as in past centuries, artists as diverse as Salvador Dali, Alberto and Diego Giacometti, Piet Mondrian and Isamu Noguchi have designed memorable furniture in this century. Within the last decade increasing numbers of artists have also turned to making chairs, tables, and cabinets. Although during the 1950s such furniture designing became regarded in some artistic circles as a lower form of creativity than painting and sculpture, recent works by Scott Burton, Donald Judd, and others have demonstrated furniture's affinity to sculpture in new ways. Much of this artists' furniture, like the whimsical items produced by Rodney Alan Greenblat and the strange, obdurate plastic laminate and wood tables of Richard Artschwager, is virtually useless: furniture *as* sculpture. Donald Judd's plain, uncompromising wooden tables and benches are uncomfortable to use, but they are clear formal extensions of his sculptural ideas.

Other artists, like Kim MacConnel, have transformed mass-produced, second hand sofas, chairs, and kitchen tables that are undistinguished relics from the 1950s and 1960s into something new with the artist's addition of riotous colors in traditionally tasteless hues. MacConnel and Robert Kushner have also converted their fascination with the flotsam and jetsam of flea market objects into lamp sculptures that are surrealistic and hilarious accretions of metal and plastic junk and everyday objects. However, they have taken care to make sure that these objects function quite as efficiently as lamps as they do as sculpture. The artist R. M. Fischer also creates lamps out of industrial parts and discards. In all these cases, furniture is both functional and sculptural, while also containing wry elements of social satire. Scott Burton, once a performance artist, now has made furniture his main form of expression. His pieces in marble, granite, ivory, and fine wood reinterpret ritualistic and traditional furniture forms. While much of Burton's work is designed expressly for public spaces, he has executed a few things for private collectors.

Whether collectors consider the work of these contemporary artists or choose to concentrate on design movements of the past, an awareness of the richness of design, and its important place among the arts, can create a more complex and satisfying art environment.

Above: *A table by Arch Connelly, mixed media with pearls.*

Top and left: *Scott Burton's "Two-Part Chaise Longue" and "Pair of One-Part Chairs," both in granite, refine furniture forms into pure sculpture.*

Opposite: *A trompe l'oeil cabinet by Piero Fornasetti is an example of furniture that approaches art.*

7

SITE-SPECIFIC ART
AND DECOR

Most of the art and objects people collect today are portable. They can be moved, rehung, regrouped to suit different and changing domestic environments. But there are also important site-specific works created by contemporary artists. Some of these become, by nature of their execution, part of the wall, ceiling, or floor. Such pieces may be lost when an interior is changed or repainted, since they can be moved only with expense or difficulty, if at all.

Christo's "Storefront," constructed in 1965 for Holly Solomon's apartment hallway, was moveable, even though it was site–specific. The wall drawings by artist Sol LeWitt are executed by the artist or his assistants directly on an existing wall, and if the wall is repainted, this version of the drawing is eradicated. While the collector is left with LeWitt's study for the piece, the large-scale version must be repainted if it is to be retained.

During the 1970s collectors Eugene and Barbara Schwartz commissioned several contemporary artists, among them Ed Baynard, Lydia Okamura, and Arlene Slavin, to paint compositions directly on the walls of the couple's Manhattan apartment. When the couple changed its interior and began to hang newly acquired works from the 1980s, the commissioned wall pieces—intended as ephemeral works by both artist and collectors—were obliterated.

Kurt Schwitters' elaborate Merzbau construction, which he built in his own house over several years during the late 1930s, burst through the downstairs ceiling. The piece was destroyed when the house was torn down. The late Gordon Matta-Clark cut through the interior (sometimes the exterior) walls of museums, abandoned houses, and collectors' homes to create the sculptural and conceptual pieces he called "Cuts." When buildings were remodelled or torn down, what remained (and could be bought by collectors and museums) was photographic documentation of the sites altered by the artist.

Richard Haas has devoted a large part of his career to the creation of murals that are *trompe l'oeil* extensions or alterations of existing interior architecture, providing cramped apartments or light-starved lofts with illusionistic classical, romantic, or modernist painted vistas that imaginatively revise the actual space and redress architectural shortcomings.

Top: *A Sol LeWitt wall drawing, 1987, from the collection of Carol and Arthur Goldberg.*

Bottom: *Christo's "Yellow Store Front," 1965, an installation formerly in the collection of Horace and Holly Solomon.*

The revival of interest in *trompe l'oeil* effects during the last decade has led to another widespread application: they function as a part of domestic decor. Artists and artisans have been employed to transform flat wall surfaces and uninspired architectural details into *faux* marble, stone, and wood finishes. While these special decorative effects are not art, they can be a sophisticated decorative addition that embellishes and enriches a domestic interior.

A collector makes a commitment to a piece of painting or sculpture that is integral to the space, since such works presuppose an acceptance of relative permanence within a particular collection. Will such additions enhance a collection? Does a site-specific piece represent the best, most characteristic or ambitious work of an artist? If, as in the case of an artist like Judy Pfaff, whose works demand major space and careful placement within the environment, a site-specific or integral work represents what the artist does, the devoted collector will find a place for it in his home.

Many of the collectors included in this book have eventually become interested in commissioning site–specific works from artists whose work they admire. Sometimes these commissions were undertaken as ways to creatively solve particular problems posed by awkward architectural situations. One couple commissioned sculptor Ned Smyth to design and execute a mosaic casing for an ungainly support column that could not be removed from a newly built gallery space in their apartment. The piece elegantly solves an architectural problem and has become a significant sculptural addition to the collection. Smyth also created a site-specific wall sculpture for a Park Avenue collector who wanted a strong and original piece to occupy a long, corridor-like wall of her living room.

Other collectors—like Chicago lawyer Gerald Elliott, who commissioned a suite of paintings by Robert Ryman which is currently touring a series of museums—want to demonstrate a particular commitment to the environmental purity of an artist's work. Most conventionally, artists have always been commissioned to paint portraits. Pop Art collector Leon Kraushaar found an unconventional way to commission a portrait when he asked Roy Lichtenstein to make a work based on Kraushaar's childhood memories. The artist produced what he called a notebook painting. Artists have also been commissioned by collectors to design furniture, ceramics, textiles, wall-coverings, and all kinds of things for household use. In many cases these opportunities have allowed artists to expand their own creative ideas and to experiment productively with unusual materials, while also often enriching the culture at large.

An appreciation and understanding of the essential nature of an artist's work is mandatory for collectors who undertake

Top and bottom: *Day and night views of a* trompe l'oeil *painting by Richard Haas, designed by the artist to screen the window of a modern Chicago apartment.*

commissions, especially of site–specific art and decor. The collector must clearly express his desires and needs to the artist he chooses, and not expect to interfere with the artist's ideas unnecessarily. The artist should respond with a project proposal that includes concept drawings and an estimate of costs. The collector may well pay more for a specific commission than for an already completed work by the artist, since a commission will often require special construction and installation considerations. Collectors should also realize that the cost of a commission will probably include a percentage paid to the artist's dealer.

When you commission a piece, you must be convinced that the artist is in control. Have faith in his abilities, and his own desires for the best possible work, and do not renege on the commitment you have made. A commissioned project can become an exciting collaboration between patron and artist with a unique creative reward at its completion.

Above: *The installation of a pair of monumental bronze doors by contemporary artist Tom Otterness required a remodelled doorway.*

Right: *Ned Smyth's mosaic casing for an existing structural column elegantly resolved an architectural dilemma.*

Above: *This entire* trompe l'oeil *interior from the mid-1970s by Richard Haas for a Manhattan apartment was an early example of art as postmodern decor.*

Left: *A Ned Smyth installation—acrylic, concrete, mosaic, silkscreen on fabric—formerly installed in the foyer of the Solomon residence.*

8
INSTALLING AND ARRANGING ART

From the Renaissance until the middle of the eighteenth century, works of art in the home were usually an integral part of the overall unity of an interior. With the advent of the Industrial Revolution, people began to have access to mass-produced objects. By the middle of the nineteenth century, through the Victorian era and until the very end of the century, in the homes of both the wealthy and the middle class, the goal seemed to be, in the words of design historian C. Ray Smith, "to fill rooms with collections—paintings, tapestries, manuscripts, and furnishings from the past." Upon walls papered with dark and opulent patterns hung a patchwork of ornately framed paintings and prints. Tabletops held cluttered groups of sculpture and various kinds of precious bibelots, and a general *horror vacuii* characterized households.

Such "skying" of pictures was abandoned in fashionable homes under the influence of interior designers like Elsie de Wolfe and Syrie Maugham, who introduced white walls and swept away the plethora of ornaments and multiple rows of pictures in a return to a modified, neo-classical scheme of interior decoration. Modern movements in art, architecture, and design continued the trend toward radical simplification in furnishings and decor, until the conventions of the modern interior. With their stress on plain walls, spare groups of machine-like furniture, and the asymmetrical placement of a painting or two as accent, or of a single sculpture or other object on a glass table, modern homes increasingly took on the look of galleries and museums. The loft in particular—previously artists' working space—was appropriated by urban dwellers, who seized on its vast open areas and white walls as expanses for art and turned the apartment interior into a virtual art gallery.

Today, in an era of pluralistic styles, there are no rigid rules for the placement of art in domestic surroundings. Even modernism is considered a period style by now. And many collectors have out of necessity repeated an almost Victorian massing of pictures as their collections grow and wall space shrinks.

Color

There are certainly no simple or hard-and-fast answers to questions of color when it comes to choosing, installing, and arranging art in the home. (See Chapter 14, "Using Professionals," for more on color in terms of decor and background.)

One of the first processes of education is color recognition and differentiation. When a mother turns the pages of her child's first reader, she will say, "Look at the red light." Another page, and she says, "Look at the red fire engine." Still another: "Look at the red flower." Then turning to the child, the mother asks, "Now what color is this?" The child replies, "Red!" and the loving parent responds with warmth and affection at this display of intelligence.

Most people raised and educated in the civilized world learn color in this fashion. A fixed concept of matching and recognizing color is codified in us at the earliest age as part of our ethnic, social, and cultural heritage. Yet very few get beyond that concept. The process of putting together color in original and significant ways is one of the most demanding abilities our intelligence can exercise. When collecting and living with art, color is the first attribute that becomes boring if not used well. The eye becomes accustomed to color with such ease and adaptation that unless an object's colors have strength, inventiveness, and liveliness, the object is likely to lose its visual energy. Most outstanding artists, in order to go beyond our "civilized" method of childhood color education, look to other sources for a freer sensibility—nature, art of the past, and crafts of more "primitive" societies with no such formal education.

When collecting, an understanding of color is part of becoming informed about the art that interests one. When you are hanging and arranging your art, you may, as your familiarity and knowledge become more sophisticated, want to amplify or overstate a color; or you may want to isolate a color. In time, you will gain a sense of those properties and relationships of color that are part of the artist's creative process—such as saturation, shape and pattern, juxtaposition, and, perhaps most important for the collector, durability. As a general guideline, one should try not to fight the aesthetic of the artist.

Once when Holly Solomon was hanging a Lichtenstein in bright yellow against a gold wall, Andy Warhol encouraged her to do so despite her reservations about the combination. His reasoning: "Anything goes with anything."

Symmetry and Asymmetry

Strict symmetry in the arranging of things is the most formal way to hang pictures or to display objects, and it can require a lavish expenditure of space. Small drawings and paintings may be asymmetrically grouped together on a wall within an imaginary symmetrical rectangle to unify objects of different sizes and shapes. Such an arrangement combines a dynamic sense of wall space with an organized, overall plan.

Large and important paintings also may profit from centered

Above: *A vividly patterned library wall painted by Kim MacConnel becomes the background for a romantic landscape by William Wegman.*

Left: *A stand by Kim MacConnel with casually stacked artworks serves both as display area and room divider.*

hanging, since it gives each picture an appropriate sense of importance on the wall. But works need not be "paired" just because of shape or size.

In one of the most spectacular collections presented in this book (see Chapter 25), a collection housed in an architecturally spare apartment, the walls of the hallway have been packed with drawings and paintings with no consideration of symmetrical hanging, or any other appropriate scheme. The pictures demand all the space there is and do not suffer from their crowded quarters; the halls are the designated zones for smaller works, while larger canvases are hung in roughly symmetrical groupings in the living room.

By hanging things off-center, or asymmetrically, pictures may be accommodated around large pieces of furniture or an architecturally problematic section of wall.

There is no one best solution when hanging an art collection. Considerations of period style, architectural limitations, and personal preference are what should guide each collector in making decisions. Perhaps the best guideline is an understanding of the artist's or art work's aesthetic intention and inherent qualities.

Large Paintings in Small Spaces

There are essentially three varieties of scale for paintings: the miniature, the easel picture, and the mural. Miniature or small paintings or drawings can be stacked or hung side by side; or sometimes one small painting can command a wall of its own. Easel-size paintings can also be stacked, or they can be spread around the room, individually or in groupings of particularly interesting combinations.

Modern painters have worked in increasingly large-scale formats, and today's collector of contemporary painting has the option of ever more enormous canvases. Such large works demand a major commitment on the part of the collector. While there are many who simply do not have the lavish space for such paintings, large pictures can work surprisingly well in small spaces if they are considered virtually as walls in themselves. Large sculptures can also be accommodated if the collector is willing to give up some of his living space to the work of art and does not care if it is grouped tightly with his furniture.

The undifferentiated space of a loft is one of the better habitats for larger works of art, even massive pieces of furniture.

Opposite: *A gallery installation shows the variety of forms of contemporary art that can be combined in a collection.*

Above left: *This arrangement of paintings by Italian painter Pomodoro and of various antiquities demonstrates symmetrical placement and strict centering.*

Above right: *A pair of early twentieth century American still-lifes in simple symmetrical arrangement.*

Left: *A diversified collection of twentieth century furniture and art in asymmetrical arrangement.*

One might think the combination of such works would be overpowering, but in fact the installation can create an exciting cross-current of energy, enlivening rather than confusing the space.

By creating tight groupings of furniture, large sculptures can be accommodated in the ordinary-size living room or library. Some collectors group several sculptures together in horizontal alignment without "homogenizing" the interest of individual pieces.

The point of large paintings in small spaces is that you don't always have to be concerned with seeing the painting as you would in a gallery or museum, where display is the only purpose of the room. You do not live in a gallery or museum! You live in your home, and you can put a painting on any wall it will fit, and then assemble your furniture in a utilitarian arrangement to make the room usable. Even stacking works on the floor, something you would never see in a museum, can be a perfectly acceptable solution to limited wall space (Holly Solomon finds that "it makes me think"). If you desire to live with large sculpture, don't mourn the space lost; think of the art as adding dimension to the room.

Always remember that you are *living* with art. This is your home, and the art should work as a living experience wherever you choose to put it. Even site-specific work has its options. The functional rooms of your house or apartment can display art without homage to the strict considerations of an art institution. It comes down to personal choice—both in the quality of the art and in its mode of display. If you prefer a deliberate, obviously intentional hanging, fine. If you prefer a more cavalier approach, use it. Only you can determine how your art is to be most fortuitously arranged.

The size and materials of Ned Smyth's and Brad Davis's collaborative landscape construction, "The Garden," make it an architectural element of the room.

Above: *Museum-scale modern works fill the hallway of this Manhattan apartment.*

Below: *Judy Pfaff's three-dimensional wall construction in the hallway of Holly Solomon's apartment.*

Right: *Special shelving was installed to accomodate this large collection of small sculpture and folk art.*

Below: *Two tabletop arrangements of West African folk art in the collection of Thomas Wheelock.*

52

A plain plaster wall is backdrop for a whimsical installation of American folk art.

9
SPATIAL AWARENESS

The rooms in which we live and which serve simultaneously as containers and backdrops for our possessions are more often than not rectangular boxes—two-dimensional surfaces enclosing space. Ceilings may be high or low, arched, domed or flat, but the basic parameters of available space are similar. There are walls on which to hang pictures or install shelves for objects; some are flat, others have recesses. Floors hold furniture and sculpture. Mobiles are suspended from ceilings to turn and sway with changing currents of air. An awareness of spatial properties will help the collector integrate individual paintings, sculptures, and pieces of furniture into an individually appropriate environment.

Although most paintings, drawings and other works on paper are conceived as squares or rectangles, artists have periodically experimented with shaped canvases that defy the conventional four-sided format. A circular painting by Robert Delauney, a curvilinear "Indian Bird" painting by Frank Stella, a lyric and eccentrically shaped Elizabeth Murray, or some of Ellsworth Kelly's monochromatic, geometric pieces—crisp and overpowering expanses of color and edge—all require an unusually generous amount of wall space for display and, often, considerable space out from the wall. Certain large and intricately structured pieces—a three-dimensional wall-piece by Stella or John Chamberlain, or a construction by Judy Pfaff—actually protrude aggressively into the room. These pieces demand area as well as surface, and they do not take kindly to being crowded by other pictures hung in close proximity. Unless rooms are exceptionally large, such pieces need a wall to themselves. But more usually, paintings and framed works do not protrude into the room. They can be hung over chairs, tables, sofas and the like without danger of close passage or risk of damage.

Most free-standing, three-dimensional sculptures ideally deserve enough space all around so they can be examined from all sides. Exceptions would be flat or two-dimensional sculptures that could be positioned near a wall or on a mantel or shelf, and thereby add a three-dimensional aspect to the wall's composition of art when viewed in full perspective.

An awareness of furniture as permutations of three-dimensional forms—whether considering tables, lamps, chairs, bureaus, desks, cabinets, or any visible item of living con-

venience—allows a collector to create an individual decor that can enhance his works of art. We have already taken up furniture as form, but here, in considering the spatial properties and requisites of a room, posing certain questions may be useful. How does the bulk or ornateness of a piece of furniture function formally? Does one prefer a few massive items or more delicate, airy chairs and tables? Do certain small objects require built-in cases for display—cases that, like close-standing sculpture, add depth to an essentially two-dimensional wall surface?

Textures in materials—wood, metal, fabrics—also have a dimensional aspect for the collector to consider when planning his or her environment. Thick, heavy, or patterned curtain materials, for example, can clash with the stark compositions of abstract painting. The collector of contemporary art may prefer simple window shades or curtains made from thinner, more translucent fabric. One collector who originally put up quite elaborate, shirred silk Roman shades as backdrop for paintings by Morris Louis and Roy Lichtenstein eventually replaced them with very plain flat shades. The first window treatment had not only distracted from the art, it had also aggressively encroached on the paintings. In some cases, no window shades or curtains may be desirable. Light and untrammeled view (whether daytime or clear night) can add depth and enhance the perspective of a room's art. Or the windows themselves, "unframed," can be integral to an artistic composition.

Spatial awareness—more often than not gained through self-education and experimentation—becomes an important facility for the collector, an aid to both comfort and display.

Opposite: *Two corner installations of sculpture showing three-dimensional form fitting with furniture.* Left: *Betty Woodman's ceramic interpretation of a pitcher is juxtaposed with the linear purity of a triangular paper construction by Dorothea Rockburne.* Right: *The curving mass of the grand piano contrasts with the abstract shape of a bronze figurative sculpture and lends depth to the perspective of fixtures and painting.*

Opposite top: *An Andy Warhol portrait installed in the deep space of a passageway becomes part of a stylistically diverse group of differently shaped contemporary works.* Opposite bottom: *Judy Pfaff's "undersea" wall composition explodes into a baroque profusion of forms that extend into an apartment dining room.* Above: *Simple, oversized furniture acts as a foil for a diversity of two- and three-dimensional artworks and antiquities.*

10

OTHER ROOMS
AND SPECIAL AREAS

Every room, every space in the house can be a display area for works of art. Art does not have to be confined to the living and dining rooms alone. The only rule that should govern the placement of art in the home is that the installation be appropriate to and respectful of the work of art.

While it might be modest of one to hang a Kandinsky drawing in the bathroom, such a choice would disregard the fragility of paper and ink. The steam, water vapor, and extremes of temperature and humidity generated in bathrooms can be damaging to prints, drawings, paintings, or photographs. A better place for such works is a foyer or passageway, where they also will not be damaged by direct daylight.

Some collectors have found that works done in glazed tile, like the colorful, patterned compositions by American artist Joyce Kosloff, are effective in bathrooms or kitchens, since they are not subject to water damage and can easily be cleaned. Holly Solomon commissioned a young artist to use vinyl as a material for a site-specific work in an apartment bathroom. She solved the dilemma of the kitchen by commissioning Doreen Gallo to cover walls, cabinets, and table with exuberantly colored tiles in irregular and abstract patterns, then chose the kitchen as the place to hang Roy Lichtenstein's red and yellow enamel plaque of a hot dog.

Anything hung in a kitchen should be under glass so that it can be conveniently and safely cleaned. Bathrooms and kitchens can also be used to display small bronze or metallic sculpture, or ceramics.

Foyers, when ceilings are relatively high, can be excellent and unusual places to display free–standing or hanging sculpture. So can stairwells. A Miami collector of contemporary art created a dramatic effect by suspending a large, vertically oriented, relatively light, aluminum sculpture from the ceiling of the second floor of his house, at the top of a circular staircase. It occupies the curving, double–height space formed by the stairs.

Hallways can be galleries in themselves if they are long and wide enough. They can accommodate even relatively large sculptures and paintings as in the case of Agnes Gund's apartment hall, one of the largest spaces in an apartment given over entirely to art. Smaller hallways have the advantage, mentioned before, of usually being insulated from direct sunlight, or not containing lots of furniture. Paintings demanding more space can be hung floor-to-ceiling in such spaces, as can smaller works on paper.

Bedrooms are choice places for art. While some collectors prefer to install more personal pieces in these more private rooms, others have chosen aggressive, even surprisingly powerful paintings for bedroom walls. The master bedroom is often the place collectors choose for their favorite or more fragile works—things they want to look at early and late in the day. It is also a good place for groups of small objects. In certain cases, even bedroom furnishings reflect a coherent carrying out of the overall aesthetic theme of the collection.

One might want to think twice about placing fragile works of art in children's rooms. Children themselves, as soon as they are old enough to understand, should be consulted on the selection of art for their rooms, and be allowed to decide what appeals to them out of various durable possibilities. Plexiglass-covered pictures are preferable to those framed with glass, since glass is so highly breakable. If you are hanging pictures that

Opposite above: A graffiti crib painted by Keith Haring and an assortment of powerful contemporary paintings make this dining room a distinctive environment for art.

Opposite below: Large shelf unit provides display area and serves as wall divider for dining area in a California collector's house.

Below: A collector's bathroom wall displays Joyce Kosloff's ceramic tile composition.

are glazed, put them out of reach of the kids. Children also enjoy displaying things they have made and posters they have selected.

Libraries, while mainly devoted to books and, more and more these days, to the proliferating masses of electronic gear that seem necessary to modern life, lend themselves to the display of art of all kinds. People have even hung pictures over the books on the bookshelves, and bookshelves themselves make a convenient setting for small objects and pictures casually placed. The Italian poet, Gabriele D'Annunzio, made his library into a tour de force of objects, where every horizontal and vertical surface was piled high with antique sculpture, drawings, and fragments: even the books became bases for sculpture.

The depth of the passion for collecting is taken to an extraordinary extreme in the following description of the apartment of the eighteenth century Parisian collector, Bonnier de la Mosson, from Maurice Rheim's *The Strange Life of Objects*. It demonstrates to what extent collections can take over every kind of domestic space.

The first room was a laboratory, full of gilt and marble with two fountains set back into niches and several shelves on which were arranged a series of alembics, containers, and matrasses made of English crystal; . . . next came the apothecary's room, comprising several rows of jars on cupboards . . . The third room was furnished with the strangest odds and ends; the fourth was for drugs, with bottles placed on glass-fronted shelves. It also contained . . . a number of foetuses, snakes, and other rare animals, with drawers round the bottom of the shelves holding metals, marcasites, marbles, agates, and other stones. Be-

Above: *A custom-designed kitchen for a New York loft accomodates works by Al Held and Man Ray and the pure forms of a Mies van der Rohe chair.*

Right: *Virtually the entire surface area of Holly Solomon's kitchen—walls, cabinets, and counters—was covered by artist Doreen Gallo with brightly colored tiles, glass, and stones.*

hind these two rooms a small corridor had been contrived where several human cadavers were kept, some of them with diseased parts.

The fifth room . . . was infinitely larger and higher, and was given over to natural history. The sixth room was for mechanics. Shelves with displays of machines and wooden or cardboard models relating to hydraulics, artillery, navigation, and architecture were ingeniously placed to rest on the off-shoots or branches of some wide central columns, carved as palm trees. . . . There were also several Chinese and foreign diagrams and devices: a finer gilded globe on a revolving axis occupied the center of the room. Finally the last room in the suite contained a library of rare and unexpected books covering the most diffuse subjects . . . and across a large table or bureau in the middle was spread a varied collection of shells of every kind. . . .

The rooms on the ground floor were distinguished by their splendid furniture, paintings, china, and bronzes, by an organ-chest and a show-case with a model of the Opera sets.

Such an eighteenth century cabinet of curiosities has by now become outdated, more the province of the museum than of the private collector. Few contemporary collectors could afford such eccentricity or lavish use of space, though they may still tend to amass things in series or categories.

So, no room need be immune from art. Every wall of the house can itself be a composition, taking into account shape, scale, and color—of furniture as well as art works—when composing each display area. As long as art and objects are treated with respect and care, any place is a fine place for displaying them.

Above: *A home office features Robert Motherwell's "Diary of a Painter."*

Right: *A formal nineteenth century library restored to period elegance.*

Above: *Art continues into the hallways of two apartments: draped painted fabric glows with chandelier illumination, and the smaller works of a major collection are displayed in close-fitted arrangement.*

Right: *A small but powerful painting by George Baselitz is reflected in the mirrored closet doors of a New York collector's bedroom.*

Top left: *A Fornasetti cabinet combines art and utility in this intimate bedroom.*

Above: *Any part of the home can be used for display. Here stair treads are pedestals for a folk-art collection of dog doorstops.*

Left: *The young son of a Chicago collector has an installation by Texas artist Vernon Fischer in his room. The diving planes are part of the piece.*

11
MASTERPIECES

When Vincent Van Gogh's limpid painting of irises was recently sold at auction for nearly fifty million dollars, a wistful remark made the rounds of the art world: "What will happen when one of Van Gogh's masterpieces comes up for sale?" Historically, a masterpiece was conceived to be the fully resolved, fully finished piece of work a craftsman or artist executed to demonstrate that he was skilled enough to be confirmed as member of a guild. Over time, the term has been blunted and generalized to signify any more than ordinary example of an artist's talent and skill, or to describe works by a famous or admired artist. These days even sketches by such noted figures—never meant for display outside the studio—may be regarded as masterpieces of the genre.

It is much easier to find a consensus on masterpieces among older works of art and craftsmanship ratified by layers and generations of scholarship, criticism, and approbation. A great work of art comes to represent, and to interpret, the quintessential style and concerns of a particular historical period. Knowledge and connoisseurship are essential in order to determine which are the masterpieces within a given body of work. Collectors who concentrate on a neglected art movement may acquire with relative ease outstanding examples of the works of representative artists, but with the growing sophistication of an art market that has become global in scope, finding such overlooked or neglected areas is increasingly difficult. Recently there has been a trend toward excavating formerly arcane categories in fields once looked down upon by collectors of painting and sculpture, resuscitating the reputations of furniture designers, of American and European art potters and glass makers, and in the process unearthing pieces that may legitimately be considered small masterpieces of their genres.

If you are pursuing a collection of contemporary art, you may initially find it far from clear just what is a "masterpiece" within a body of work. Often a piece which seems incomplete or at first doesn't quite "work" (in the sense of unapparent context) will turn out to be a quintessential expression of the artist's ideas. Its very unfulfillment can lead to the development of

Above: *An untitled major work by Cy Twombly fills an entire wall.*

Opposite: *Francis Bacon's "Studies from the Human Body" in the entrance hall of a London townhouse; on a wall nearby, Picasso's "Head of a Woman" (1971).*

radical, even revolutionary concepts. That can be one of the satisfactions and more exciting attractions of collecting: to take the chance—out of your own desires, intuition, and increasing knowledge—that a work will *become* a masterpiece. And then, living with that work of art, you can be doubly rewarded, by being a participant in its rising reputation as well as recipient of its increased value.

In any genre, if one owns a piece considered or likely to be considered a masterpiece, its simultaneous protection and display can be an issue for the private collector, and sometimes a difficult one to resolve. For example, when Holly Solomon started collecting Claes Oldenburg, she had no desire to enclose the work, feeling it would diminish its textural and sculptural qualities; in time, however, she did have to encase it in a plastic box as a necessity for its preservation . . . and still regrets the loss of intimacy. (For more on the physical protection of art, see Appendix, "Conservation.") Obviously valuable pieces such as pre–Columbian gold objects are likely to require specially built glass display cases, as will delicate ceramics. Questions of insurance and security (also see Appendix) become pressing when one owns such rarities. The collector must decide whether he can afford the responsibility; if not, the work might be better off in storage or on loan to a museum.

A great painting virtually usurps pride of place in a room, no matter which wall it occupies. Its quality and energy may force less powerful or compatible art off the walls entirely. Yet this too should be subject to the experience of living with the art. "I wouldn't dare hang most contemporary paintings from the 1980s in this room," says a collector who prizes a superb Brancusi bird, a 1942 Mondrian, and a very abstract Jackson Pollock.

"I wasn't even sure the Pollock could hold up when it first got here." What she did, in essence, was use the Brancusi and the Mondrian, which she had accepted and lived with as great pieces, to test the Pollock—and it worked!

A work may be deemed a masterpiece because it sums up a particular style—it embodies a certain resolution of ideas—but its status may also be decided by the rarity of its authorship. The Cellini cup, in all its jeweled opulence, once the pride of the Metropolitan Museum, was instantly demoted in status when the experts agreed that it was not by Benvenuto Cellini at all but was instead the work of a supremely clever and gifted nineteenth century German goldsmith who had set about to create works in the style of the Renaissance. The object was the same; only its attribution had changed. Now it was a forgery, not a masterpiece.

Opposite: *Arshile Gorky's abstract painting hangs over a Hepplewhite English sideboard with nineteenth century candlesticks and contemporary chairs.*

Below: *A dining room wall holds Jasper John's 1963 "Map." Beneath it is Judy Shea's sculpture, "Acting Out," made in 1984.*

12
LIGHTING

Lighting is part of the relationship you have to the art in your home. You see your art in the morning light, in the afternoon through time of dusk, and at night. You see it far away, perhaps from the distance of other rooms, and you see it up close. You *live* with your art, and the experience is very different from that of passing through a museum or gallery, from one formally composed room to the next, each with its art works lit without regard to any considerations of living other than display.

A certain collector of oriental sculpture painstakingly installed customized lighting for his works of art. Around his dining room were at least six Cambodian bodhisattvas, each in a special niche. Framing spotlights, hidden in the ceiling and controllable by rheostats, exactly focussed on each rectangular cubicle, bathing each statue in a precise and discrete field of light. The effect was theatrical and magical, nicely suited to contrast with the dark green walls of the room. But the short-comings of the apparatus became apparent when one or another of the light fixtures deviated, even ever so slightly, from its target. Electricians had to be called in, time after time, to re-calibrate the precisely positioned lighting.

While a gallery or a museum has a professional responsibility to light each work it exhibits to provide clarity and coherence within an exhibition, the domestic lighting of art can be more adaptable to requirements of comfort and mood. As lighting designer Howard Brandston has pointed out, "It is with light that art is perceived, and a contrast of lighting qualities, quantities, and focuses can make a place stimulating or fatiguing." If domestic lighting is too bright or monotonous, it can create museum fatigue at home. This is often the case for new collectors of modern art as they try to approximate the wash of bright light found in contemporary galleries and museums.

This is not to deny that there are issues specific to lighting works of art in the home. Different paintings need different consideration. For example, a Mark Rothko or a reflective gold painting by Yves Klein can not be directly lighted—it spoils the effect of the painting by overemphasizing the brush strokes and other technical details. Such paintings need little light to radiate. For other paintings—and this would apply as well to any vertically displayed, two-dimensional subject, including prints and photographs—the collector should decide whether he wants overall, uniform light, only lighted surfaces, or only

Above: *A fish lamp by architect Frank Gehry serves both as sculptural fantasy and working light fixture.*

Opposite top: *A massive skylight in a California collector's home at once allows substantial daylight and leaves unobstructed wall display space for art. Ceiling spotlights augment the ambient light.*

Opposite bottom: *In a New York apartment, a Robert Motherwell painting receives illumination from both ceiling spotlights and ambient side-lighting.*

Right: *The scintillating materials used by Thomas Lanigan-Schmidt in this bedroom niche reflect and enhance the table lighting.*

Below: *A progression from generous ambient light to a dramatically darkened passageway provides contrast for a shaped canvas by Catherine Porter.*

Below right: *Small recessed spotlights eccentrically placed in the ceiling of this Paris apartment provide an unusual lighting solution in keeping with the apartment's overall design.*

Opposite top left and right: *Backlit shelves supply theatrical illumination for a collection of modern Italian glass; a focussed spotlight emphasizes the rich materials of a Bugatti-designed shelf, which appears to be dramatically backlit.*

Opposite bottom left and right: *Ceiling spotlights illuminate a painting by Ed Paschke and highlight the sheen of a group of architect-designed silver tea services; a painted glass dome by Richard Haas imitates an exterior view and filters natural light.*

lighted pictures. Often, ambient light will have to be augmented by focused light to enhance the paintings. Such specific spotlights can be adjusted to add warmth and color to the lighting.

Light usually has to reveal the mass, plasticity, and surface detail of sculpture and other three–dimensional objects. This may require two sources of light, as well as some adjustment of the color of the light. For example, a sculpture could be placed by a window with a spotlight directed at the other side. Occasionally, you might actually want to keep an object in shadow or even darkness—imagine the excitement of a Rodin in silhouette!

Lighting for art is simply one aspect of lighting for the home and should be considered within the context of your overall requirements for efficient and pleasant artificial light. One sensible approach is to think of your domestic surroundings as a sequence of experiences: arrival, patterns of use in each room, and departure. Generally speaking, lighting should follow the practical logic of your customary needs, of how you use your house or apartment. After those patterns have been satisfied, other lighting needs specific to your art can be planned.

One can study how other people light their homes, taking notes or even polaroid pictures as reminders of particular lighting solutions. Remember too that architects and other home-design experts don't necessarily take lighting into account. When working with such professionals, clients should insist on being shown examples of suggested lighting solutions before any built-in lighting is installed. Lighting designers point out that homeowners usually tend to overlight their houses or apartments.

While overall, good lighting in a home will sufficiently illuminate works of art, there are special lighting considerations for collectors. Extravagant lighting solutions such as expansive built-in systems can cost as much as the art itself and will require extensive construction and remodeling. Certain collectors plan in advance where large works, or sculptures difficult to move, will be placed on permanent display, and will build precisely directed spotlighting to highlight these works while they are renovating. Track lighting, first used in display, store, and theatrical lighting, can supply a number of fixtures placed at various points along a length of track fitting. Though it has the

virtues of being flexible and relatively inexpensive, track lighting is at this point still a somewhat primitive solution. It can also be obtrusive architecturally and hardly fits in with older styles of interior architecture. Indirect lighting, provided by fixtures with baffles or soffits, can be directed down from the ceiling or up from floor fixtures to wash walls (and pictures) with a general flow of light. Traditional picture lights which attach to picture frames are a common method of lighting art, but they are apt to seem pretentious and awkward appendages and are usually suitable only for older paintings.

Tungsten-halogen lamps provide very small, concentrated sources of light and large quantities of light, and are useful for indirect lighting, though special care must be used to avoid their powerful glare. These lights also produce high levels of heat and should not be placed too near a work of art. Certain light fixtures, like the lamps designed by Frank Gehry and Alberto Giacometti, are design objects in their own right, more notable for their interesting shapes and forms than for the quality of light they emit. Such objects can be incorporated into a room as decorative accents, rather than as primary light sources.

The satisfying and efficient use of artificial light is usually a matter of trial and error for the collector, depending on the effect he wishes to create. Natural daylight is another issue, for sunlight, while the best illumination, is the enemy of art. Collectors must determine which of their works need to be protected from natural light, as well as from humidity, heating outlets, and airborne polutants such as dust. Many collectors rotate fragile drawings, prints, and photographs, displaying them for limited periods of time, or they hang them in areas which receive only indirect daylight.

What we have given you in this chapter amount to guidelines and suggestions. There are really no rules about lighting your home. If you wish to duplicate a museum or gallery experience, you should consult a professional. And if you desire an ambience which involves special light fixtures for your art, try to achieve it without letting the art compromise your normal or preferred way of life. Always remember that this is your home—yours in which to decide what to highlight or not highlight. You have no public curatorial responsibility to display your treasures, but only to be happy in their company.

Opposite left: *A variety of simple wood, metal, and gilded frames protect but do not overwhelm the art in this concentrated installation.*

Opposite right: *A Brad Davis painting elaborately matted and simply framed in singular mantel display.*

13
ISSUES
OF FRAMING

Museums have curators, conservators, and conservation studios to consider the aesthetic and archival questions that are part of caring for and displaying works of art, but private collectors rarely begin with any knowledge of these issues. Nevertheless, they are a crucial part of collecting. There are important considerations to be aware of when framing works of art.

It is imperative that the collector work with a reputable framer, for the field is fraught with destructive practices that result from ignorance and lack of training. A gallery or museum you trust may be a source for finding a good framer. But you must know what questions to ask when you need glazing and framing.

Insuring the utmost archival and physical stability for a work should be the collector's first concern. It should also be the framer's. "Collectors must be aware that heat, light, and humidity are the foremost enemies of art, especially of works on paper," says Manhattan frame-maker Brooke Larsen. "Any framing must protect art from these destructive elements in so far as it is possible." The collector must ask the framer whether he uses acid-free and ultra-violet resistant materials when matting and glazing works on paper, including photographs. It is best to talk to the framer before you bring any art into his shop. If you feel he is not going to be satisfactory you won't be tempted to leave the art with him to save yourself the trouble of carrying it home.

Framer Jared Bark, who is known for his innovative, plain wooden frames for contemporary art, points out that conservators used to include frames with all the other natural enemies of art. "Most people," he says, "are interested in the decorative aspects of frames and disregard the conservation issues." In recent years, technical advances have made safer framing more widely available.

Considerations are somewhat different for unglazed works (paintings on canvas) and works on paper. Frames used for paintings should never touch or abrade the canvas. Instead, they should be separated from the surface of the picture by a buffer

material. Conventional strip frames (used on larger paintings) can twist and warp with climatic changes. Framers recommend a stronger and more stable system such as a float frame that can be screwed to the painting stretcher. "Don't assume that a gallery or even the artist framed something in the right way," cautions Brooke Larsen.

Jared Bark distinguishes between the matting, glazing, and framing of works on paper. He recommends the use of nothing less than eight- or twelve-ply, acid-free mats, stressing that the mat must be thick enough to keep any work on paper as far away from glazing materials as possible. "Unsized papers, used by many contemporary artists, are very floppy," he points out. They can substantially expand and contract in different climate conditions. (Remember that linen and silk mats are not archival.) Also recommended is the use of four-ply 100% rag board or chemically purified woodpulp cardboard for backing works.

One of the most destructive framing elements can be the adhesives and hinges used to attach a work to a backing material. Hinging paste should be made of rice or wheat flour and pure water. Very large works are sometimes attached by using expensive polyester mesh. "I would not use a framer who, when asked about what kind of hinges he uses, says linen and not usually rice paper," says Bark. "You don't want him learning how to hinge with rice paper on your art work." Linen hinges, acceptable for hinging mats, tend to adhere and yellow, leaving marks on works on paper. Many stronger adhesives such as pressure–sensitive tapes also discolor and cannot be removed. Some framers employ mylar corners to hold photographs in place.

A popular and inexpensive method for framing posters has been dry mounting, but this solution destroys the work and should definitely be avoided. No work of art should ever be cut or folded to fit a mat or a frame.

Since the cardinal rules of conservation-quality framing are that no materials should damage the art work and nothing done should be irreversible, frames should protect works from environmental problems. Glazing with glass is cheaper than using ultra violet resistant plexiglass, but there is no glass that shields from u–v rays. (Denglas, manufactured by Denton Vacuum Company, has a crystalline coating that makes it virtually non-reflective, but it does not shield from u–v rays.) The virtues of glass are that it doesn't scratch and is relatively free of distortion and defects, along with its more economical qualities. Its liabilities are that it breaks easily and its color tints can distort the colors of a work. Plexiglass is lightweight, hard to break, scratches easily, and creates static cling. No copy machine-generated works, photographs or fragile pastels should be glazed with plexiglass, since static can pull the pigment or photo-

graphic emulsions from the paper to the frame. Plexiglass can be treated to resist u–v rays, but this is more than twice as expensive as using glass.

Recommended reading for the archival fine points of framing artworks is *The Care and Handling of Art Objects, Practices in The Metropolitan Museum of Art,* available from the museum or from Harry N. Abrams, Publishers.

After archival considerations come the aesthetics of framing. Many artists create their own frames as extensions of the particular art work. These should never be removed. If necessary, the entire work, including the original frame, can be reframed in a glass or plexiglass container for protection. Ideally, frames added by galleries, collectors, or museums should respect the intent of the artist. One should think carefully before removing any frame installed in a previous period, since the frame itself may reflect an added cultural richness from that period. When The Museum of Modern Art "down-framed" its permanent collection in the course of reinstallation, the reaction of the art community was highly critical. By removing the diversity of formal and cultural influences reflected in the diversity of frames, the Museum imposed a dictatorial aesthetic upon its works of art.

Aesthetic framing decisions depend on sensitivity to the work itself, sensitivity to its materials, period of origination, and existence as an object independent of decor. Don't compromise frames to make them match a particular decor. One collector wished to tint white some beautiful cherry wood frames that surrounded certain delicate Cy Twombly studies. His framer convinced him to desist, since altering them would have ruined the contrasting edge of the frame and since the wood itself would never have accepted the proposed finish.

There have been design innovations and revivals in framing over the past three decades. Robert Kulicke pioneered the aluminum section frame so prominent on works of the late 1960s and early 1970s. He also created a line of innovative plexiglass box frames. During the 1970s, Jared Bark developed a plain, squared wood frame. More elaborate varieties of frames have come back into vogue in the 1980s, including the wide-faced wooden frame (often colored) so popular in the nineteenth century and now favored by artists like Mark Innerst and Neil Jenney.

Proper framing is likely to be expensive. It can also take time, and the framer should not be rushed on a job. A good frame for a small work on paper will rarely cost less than $75, and it could be as much as $200. Most small or local framers are not archivally trained, nor do they have access to a qualified restorer (if that is a consideration). Too many have outdated or insufficient general knowledge of correct procedures and materials. So it is best to ask very specific questions, or to consult with clearly more expert framers accustomed to dealing with contemporary works. Even if they charge a consulting fee, the resulting knowledge can be well worth the money. European framers, while versed in traditional craftsmanship and antique techniques, are not as archivally careful nor as technically sophisticated as their American counterparts. Collectors who learn archival techniques and who are aware of the complexities of framing will be able both to care for their art and to make appropriate choices for its display.

Modest, even severely plain framing serves a trio of modern paintings.

A gallery of contemporary art with integral framing . . .

Clockwise, starting upper left: *"U.N. Plaza" by Richard Artschwager, cellotex on canvas; "Akumal" by Marcia G. King, oil on canvas with elaborate multi-media frame; Izhar Patkin's "Vertigo," photostat with scrim and embroidery on wood; "Hula Girl" by Kim MacConnel, acrylic on canvas with painted wood frame.*

Clockwise, starting upper left: *Brad Davis's "Seascape," acrylic on canvas with polyester frame; "Geometriche Absurd" by Willy van Sompel, dayglo paint and glitter with wood frame; a multi-media foil construction by Thomas Lanigan-Schmidt, encased in plexiglass; "The Cock and the Lemon" by Izhar Patkin, oil on screen with pebble frame; untitled by Neil Jenney, acrylic on canvas with wood frame.*

14
USING PROFESSIONALS

A major point we have been trying to stress, and will illustrate by example in the next part of this book, is that while art may serve as part of the decor of a home, good art is never merely decorative. Still, many collectors do turn to professional decorators, interior designers, and architects to help them develop the setting for their objects and pictures as well as to aid in the arrangements and juxtapositions of furniture, paintings, and sculpture. The responsibility for the success or failure of such collaborations rests ultimately with the client. If you do choose to work with a professional, it is crucial that you proceed with a clear grasp of your desires and priorities.

One prominent New York decorator who designed her own apartment around a spectacular collection of modern paintings finds that a majority of collectors "are basically very timid." They feel apprehensive about color and usually insist that nei-

ther wall colors nor curtains and furniture stray from a bland neutrality. "Everyone wants white walls and beige sofas and curtains," she says. "They cannot imagine a more daring color scheme and usually avoid dark or bright wall colors which actually can enhance the display of paintings."

Although artists, galleries, and museums are beginning to set up installations that use wall colors in more daring and creative ways, the popular predilection for white or grey walls stems to a degree from the utilitarian needs of the gallery system. Because art galleries are constantly rehanging paintings, they generally prefer white walls for being so advantageous to upkeep and repair. When it comes to the home, however, the choice of wall color should be based on what pleases the homeowner. Different colors please different people, and you should be guided in the main by what makes you feel good or seems most becoming to you and your style of life. The use of a room and its frequency of use can be helpful clues. For instance, in a dining room used infrequently you can be dramatic or bold. In your bedroom, on the other hand, you may want to chose something calming or comforting. If you like pattern walls or fabrics, see how the artworks co-exist; there's a wide range of choices. Of course, decor and artworks shouldn't fight, but neither has to overrule or "dictate" the other. Your home is where

An apartment designed by architect Michael McDonough, and another by designer Richard Hare.

you live, and the objects in it should be based on personal affection.

Some knowledge or at the least awareness of the decorative arts can be useful to the art collector. Sensitivity to quality in the design of anything from major pieces of furniture to items such as china, light fixtures, and fabrics enhances the environment of a collection. A wise alternative may be to seek out a qualified dealer well schooled in the decorative arts and committed to acquiring authentic examples rather than whipping up copies in a workshop. A good dealer will inform and teach you about the objects that most attract you. But don't rush. You are better off acquiring gradually than buying things *en suite*.

While authentic furniture and good art always make a strong statement in an interior, it is important to remember that arranged things do affect one another in juxtapositions that can be either jarring or compatible to varying degrees. A good designer can help in organizing the arrangements of rooms in ways that will enhance both objects and pictures.

Some professionals are more interested in how a room may look on the magazine page than in how it actually works (and some collectors, welcoming possible publicity, might well want such an approach). The collector should scrutinize previous examples of a decorator's work to find out where its focus lies. The best decorators will understand how to create intimacy and variety using texture, scale, color, and form to create a satisfying whole. They will also appreciate the installation needs of a collection. For example, if art is rotated often, fabric walls may reduce the frequency of repainting. Collectors of contemporary art also usually require high ceilings to accomodate their oversized pieces. A decorater who recommends lowering the ceilings is working at odds with such a collection.

A good decorator functions as an inspired organizer, refining the display and arrangement of things, simplifying clutter or pulling space together through color, so that it better sets off the art. He can also, like a good dealer, supply information that makes the decor more meaningful.

Never be afraid to question a decorator's reasons for suggesting certain solutions, and insist on an overall plan. You don't want your apartment or house "done" so that it fails to allow for growth, change, and spontaneity. And don't let your decorator, designer, or architect overimpress you. These experts are supposed to help you find yourself, and by being fearful of resisting or arguing against their prescriptions you will not be helping either yourself or them in the main task: to make an environment that suits *you*.

Part Two
Environments

15
A MARRIAGE OF ART AND DESIGN

"Pictures, drawings, and objets d'art all have personalities of their own." Jacques Guignard

The unusual, two-level ground floor of an old Manhattan townhouse is the architectural setting for this extremely sophisticated collection of contemporary art and decorative-art objects from the 1940s and 1950s. The art that is skyed on the white-painted brick walls and tucked under the sweeping staircase, also into the large front hall and around the tiny balcony sitting room, has been acquired gradually over a period of nearly thirty years. The collection began with the acquisition of a small, green Jasper Johns target painting in 1957 and has continued to grow with paintings and sculpture from the past three decades. Cy Twombly, Jim Dine, Frank Stella, Victor Vasarely, Josef Albers, and Ad Reinhart are some of the older artists represented in the collection. Carl Andre, Brice Marden, Robert Morris, David Novros—artists whose reputations came of age during the 1960s—hang beside the much more recent works of Robert Wilson, Robert Mapplethorpe, David Salle, Julian Schnabel, Mike Bidlo, Jean-Michel Basquiat, and Francesco Clemente.

The collector, for whom the visual arts have been a passion for thirty years, says she acquires "emotively" and that the desire to own a work comes "rarely and suddenly." Otherwise, she has been content to let art remain "part of the general visual field that is my public and professional life." The highly personal selection demonstrated in this collection serves as a record of the stylistic changes in art of the recent past, a barometer of advanced artistic efforts in our time.

The collection's recent concentration on the furniture and decorative arts of the 1940s and 1950s began only a few years ago with the acquisition of Isamu Noguchi's classic kidney-shaped table that now holds a selection of Italian ceramics from the 1950s and a group of tiny relief sculpture by California sculptor Robert Graham. The collector attribes this shift to her response to the painting of the early 1980s which allowed her to connect conceptually and integrate the sinuous designs of objects by Charles Eames, Noguchi, Carlo Mollino, and Vladimir Kagan (whose enormous, eccentrically curving grey sofa is the major piece of furniture in the living room and was acquired from the designer himself) with contemporary art and with such strong items of contemporary design as the fish lamp and the cardboard chairs by California architect Frank Gehry.

Unlike many recent collections of "modern" design, this one has nothing to do with sentimental nostalgia for 1950s popular culture. Each object, including lamps, vases, ashtrays and light fixtures, has been selected with a highly cultivated and conscious awareness of its formal properties and of the quality of its design in terms of wit, expressiveness, and sculptural resolution. The collection has been disciplined and refined to exclude any aspects of kitsch. As such, it can never be mistaken as a static "period" statement. Instead, it is a living and evolving record of a collector's understanding that the best design, like the best art, has a life that reaches beyond any pragmatic or dated function.

Above: *A 1974 geometric canvas by David Novros contrasts with a Calder-influenced ceiling light, designed by architect Victor Gruen in the 1950s for a chain of Barton's candy stores, and two cardboard chairs by Frank Gehry.*

Opposite: *Jean-Michel Basquiat's 1980 canvas hangs over a slatted bench by George Nelson. Beyond it, a plaster Giacometti lamp throws light on Julian Schnabel's 1980 painting, "What to do with a Corner in Madrid."*

Above: *The recessed space beneath the balcony serves as a dining area. The table, designed by Donald Desky in 1958, has been paired with chairs from the Swiss Pavillion at the 1939 World's Fair (and are still being produced 50 years later). An elegant wall piece by Donald Judd is hung next to a graphite drawing by Brice Marden.*

Opposite: *Natural light from the large picture window and the translucent glass ceiling illuminate the two-story living room. A pair of Barcelona chairs by Mies van der Rohe, a Bakuba drum, a fish lamp designed by Frank Gehry, Noguchi's famous glass coffee table, and a Robsjohns Gibbings bench are arranged with the geometric rug designed in 1929 by American painter and graphic designer E. McKnight Kauffer. Over the Kagan sofa is a 1987 painting by neo-geo artist Meyer Vaisman.*

Two views from the balcony den of this Manhattan townhouse into its double-heigh[
living room. Sculpturally shaped sidechairs by Charles Eames, Corai, Carlo Mollin[
and Ernest Race are placed with Corbusier club chairs and tables by Jens Risom, N[
guchi, and Piretti. The rug, made in the 1950s, is from Holland. On the walls are worl[
by David Salle and Dutch constructivist painter Josef Peters, drawings by Ad Rineha[
and Rory McEwen, aand a photographic composition by Robert Mapplethorpe. A si[
uous sofa originally designed and made by Vladimir Kagan for a Walter Gropius hous[
is a sculptural form as well as a major seating area in the living room under painting[
by David Salle, Joseph Albers, and Cy Twombly.

Two details of the living room. Left: Another Noguchi table holds a
collection of tiny intaglio sculptures by Robert Graham, a group of
extravagantly distorted Italian glass bottles from the fifties by Fantoni,
and a Giacometti table lamp; on the wall, paintings by Brice Marden
and Larry Poons. **Right:** Two Rietfeld "Z" chairs are pure form. The
curved side table by Risom holds a ceramic lamp from the 1956 Italian
Triennale and a Higgins glass ashtray. A black painting by Ad Reinhart hangs next to Gerhard Merz's depiction of Brazilia.

16
AN INGENIOUS APPROACH

"Artists may be said to collect with a greater sense of unity than other men, since their possessions fulfill a very precise inspirational purpose." Francine du Plessix Grey

Some thirty-five years ago, Philip Pearlstein was still an impecunious student of art history and a fledgling painter. He had just taken his comprehensive examinations in art history at New York University's Institute of Fine Arts, where he wrote his thesis on Francis Picabia. The young painter and his artist wife, Dorothy, had $200 to spare and felt like celebrating. At first they almost spent the money on a small Alberto Giacometti sculpture that they saw in New York. But a trip to California intervened, and during that trip their friend Martin Friedman (now the director of the Walker Art Center in Minneapolis) took them around to the shop of an antiquities dealer. "We saw a beautiful Greek figure of Athena, and we couldn't resist her. So that was what we spent the money on and how our collecting began," says Pearlstein. "Now the Giacometti is worth tens of thousands and our Athena—we still have it— is still worth $200! But we have no regrets."

When the Pearlsteins went to Italy in 1958 on a Fulbright grant, Philip kept on buying antiquities in Rome, carefully spending a little of his student budget. He would sometimes pick up bags of fragments of vases and restore them himself by pasting them together. "I still like fragments," says the now highly respected painter, "and I've often also bought abraded vases, one of which turned out to be quite important."

The Pearlsteins' collecting activities have continued through the years, and have gradually expanded in several directions. On his return from his Roman sojourn, Pearlstein discovered the same character of drawing that interested him in Greek vases in the cheap and plentiful Japanese prints that were still available in New York. One place he found them was at the Weyhe Bookstore and Gallery on Lexington Avenue, where there were "packages of prints that had never been unwrapped. Since we couldn't afford the fifty dollar prints, we bought many of the ten dollar ones." It was also where the painter bought many of the Piranesi prints that now hang in the vestibule of the West Side loft where he works and where the Pearlsteins currently live. Another source of Japanese prints was the Brooklyn Museum Gift Shop. Pearlstein also learned that he could often restore the prints himself. "I got two Kitagawa Utamaro prints for $125. I took them home and washed and ironed them. They turned out wonderfully."

The Pearlsteins' collection has grown over the years to include American folk art, arrestingly sculptural pieces of furniture, Eadweard Muybridge photographs, and old master prints. Since many of the objects and the benches, *chaises*, and sofas serve as props in the artist's work, he has arranged them throughout the studio part of the loft, where they are startlingly reproduced as elements in his monumental paintings of groups of reclining nude figures. The Kilim rugs the couple has collected also play a prominent part in many of the paintings.

The situation of the artist as collector is very often a special one. Making art and collecting it are intertwined in uniquely personal ways. In Pearlstein's case, his collection has served to enrich his paintings. Its objects are models, sources for ideas, and provocative images for the works. He has also been able to trade his own works for the Greek, Roman, and primitive objects which fascinate and inspire him. One of his sources for Americana has been one of his former art students from Pratt Institute, who often found desirable folk art pieces for him. Another source of knowledge was the late Willard Cummings, founder of the Skowhegan School of Painting and Sculpture, the summer art school in Maine where Pearlstein was a faculty member.

Cummings, a painter in his own right, was also a perspicacious collector of American folk art, china, and early American furniture. "His house in Maine, filled with folk art portraits, ironstone, and rugs, really helped to get us interested," Pearlstein recalls. "We did a lot of looking and buying up in Maine, in the area around Skowhegan." The Pearlsteins also credit dealers John Gordon, Edward Merrin, André Emmerich, and Lucien Goldschmidt as influential sources of knowledge and specific works. "They were generous with their knowledge and time and they were willing to let you buy things on the installment plan."

The Pearlsteins stress that they have been able to collect over the years without spending huge amounts of money. Dorothy Pearlstein, who became a teacher and then a dealer in prints, and who now works as an artistic consultant on educational and publishing projects, recalls finding real bargains at furniture auctions at Sotheby's when it was on Madison Avenue and was still Parke-Bernet. "In those days, the usual furniture auctions were very sparsely populated," she remembers. "It was much cheaper and more interesting to buy there or from the antique shops along Columbus Avenue than it was to get something new."

An American twig rocker and nineteenth century American rooster weathervane, carved decoys, and an eighteenth century spool bed with a blue-and-white woven jacquard coverlet are arranged beneath the artist's "Two Models by the Window with Cast Iron Toys" (1987). The painting is taken from the actual view and arrangements of objects on the windowsill of the loft.

American folk art, antiquities, pre-Columbian pottery, Kilim rugs, and furniture are all used by painter Philip Pearlstein in his large figure paintings, as demonstrated by two paintings completed in 1987. "Marionettes and Model" includes two American minstrel marionettes, and "Model with Swan Decoy" is a modern-day Leda with a folk art swan.

Opposite: A carved and polychromed wooden figure of Mercury that was probably used to adorn a post office is reputed to have been made near Boston in the late eighteenth century. It is displayed on a bountifully adorned table that has multiple uses.

90

For years the Pearlsteins spent Saturdays looking through the galleries on Madison Avenue, to see both current exhibitions and the antiquities and prints that interested them. Pearlstein considered the money he received for lecture fees as his "art buying fund." He has sometimes traded or sold objects in order to acquire other things. But he does not collect with any fixed idea of reselling. "I've found that if you resell to a dealer, you rarely make money," he says. "And if you put something on consignment with a dealer—especially the kind of things I'm interested in—there is rarely a concentrated effort to resell it, so it can sit for a long time."

Some collectors require that what they buy be in prime condition, and conventional advice stresses condition as a prerequisite for serious consideration. But Pearlstein doesn't mind variations in the quality of the condition of the things he gets. "The condition is not as important to me as the genius of the piece itself," he says.

The extremely varied pieces of classical, pre-Columbian, Indian and folk art that make up the core of the Pearlstein's collection are unified by the artist's eye and are a record of what nourishes and informs his own art. As such, it is a highly personal "sarcophagus of memory and knowledge."

Above: *Beautifully patterned, wood-grained cupboards provide a backdrop for the carved sculpture of a woman that may have decorated a ship's pilot house. The fish sculpture was probably a shop sign, and the metal cut-out of a fox was painted with oils. To the right, an elaborate carving by twentieth-century Northwest Coast carver Seaweed Charlie.*

Below left: *Classical objects, pre-Columbian pottery, and ancient Egyptian artifacts are grouped on top of the artist's storage cabinets.*

Right: *Two American folk art figures of horses flank an early American bench over which another of the artist's paintings is hung.*

17
A UNIFYING EYE

"A great collector must indicate a strong personal preference." Sir Kenneth Clark

William Greenspon, who was a child psychiatrist for twenty-five years, came to his second double career of private art dealer and painter through his passion for collecting. "At first, during the early sixties," he says, "I began collecting contemporary art. Then I collected antiquities, pre-Columbian art, Japanese and Chinese ceramics. In each of those areas things got progressively more expensive and I found that my taste and knowledge would inevitably outrun my pocketbook." Then Greenspon found folk art. "It captivated me just on its aesthetic merits, and I thought that I could get something significant that I could afford."

That was seventeen years ago. Now Greenspon's upper West Side Manhattan apartment is an eloquent testimonial to the successful transformation of his collection. It is filled with an eccentric, elegant, and important group of folk art objects that range from nineteenth century American sternboard figures to industrial models and Penitente figures from the Southwest. The simplified forms of Greenspon's collection of vintage Bauhaus furniture make an initially startling contrast to the primitive qualities of his objects. Further consideration of this unusual combination confirms that everything here is unified by Greenspon's deep interest in and understanding of modernism. His folk art objects relate both to the formal aspects of modernism and to the collector's abiding fascination with surrealism as a sub-category of modernism. Objects and furniture alike also demonstrate his fascination with industrial design.

A board full of wooden neckties, exquisitely inlaid with different kinds of wood, is "my poor man's Duchamp." A small stool whose seat is a mass of rubber spikes (it was used as a fraternity initiation gadget) is "a poor man's Man Ray." And, an odd, tilted cup and saucer turns out to be an industrial model with definite affinities to Meret Oppenheim's famous surrealist, fur-lined teacup. There are rubber hat models, a rubber owl, and a mirrored ax as well as several large figures and costumes. These are what Greenspon calls his "disembodied people": two baseball figures with moveable parts (1923) that once were part of a stadium concession, minstrel and pearly costumes, and a monumental tin display figure rescued from an obsolete gas station in Jewett City, Connecticut. The collector also is fond of a funeral suit, pristine in its original box, exuberantly noting its resemblance to Jim Dine's well-known bathrobe images.

Greenspon combines such anonymous industrial objects as a washing machine agitator that looks exactly like a post-cubist abstract sculpture, and an equally sculptural group of old tire molds with important eighteenth and nineteenth century portraits and one of only two known eighteenth century ship figureheads from Stonington, Connecticut. His wooden bust of Daniel Webster, from an American whaling ship, the *Daniel Webster*, which sailed out of Sag Harbor, New York, is dated from 1847. It is exceptionally rare Americana. Another unique folk art piece is the large weathervane, a model of Bleriot's plane, that once adorned the Poland Spring House in Maine. Greenspon bought it about fifteen years ago at an auction of the Huntington collection in Maine.

Greenspon's sophisticated sense of formalist values is nowhere more apparent than in his Bauhaus sofas, tables, desks and lighting fixtures. Most of his furniture has been acquired in Europe from a select number of recognized Bauhaus experts. His dining room table was designed by Mart Stam, his living room coffee table by the Dutch designer Gispen. Other pieces are by Mies van der Rohe, Michael Thonet, and Marcel Breuer. Greenspon's implicit understanding of Bauhaus design principles is demonstrated by the wall cabinets that he designed and built to hold small objects and files. The spare and practical units are made of elegantly joined, unfinished wood topped with industrial rubber, surfaces which harmonize with his period furniture.

Objects and paintings in the collection are constantly rotated in and out of storage. Greenspon says that for a long time he "just traded something for something else I wanted." Now he finds good folk art is getting harder and harder to find. "Everybody's getting smarter." He currently acquires things through a complex network of sources that includes other dealers and collectors, auctions, and pickers who call him from all over the country when they spot something they think might appeal to his distinctive tastes.

Greenspon feels that his training in modern art and his own work as a painter have immeasurably enhanced his abilities to perceive the aesthetic strengths of objects that more conventional folk art dealers might bypass. He points out that ninety percent of the dealers are trained only in folk art and antiques. "They don't have the broad reach of thought that would enable them to see some of the formal convergences that make things interesting to me," he says. He points out the affinities between nineteenth century ship carving and Roman sculpture and finds

William Greenspon's diverse folk art and examples of early industrial design harmonize with the pure lines of his Bauhaus sofa, chairs, tables, and lamps.

The pale walls of the living room are a good foil for an American farm sign, more Bauhaus furniture, a Cockney pearly costume, and an American carved skeleton, the latter two being examples of Greenspon's "disembodied people."

94

An early industrial artifact—a washing machine agitator—is used as a centerpiece for the dining room table designed by Mart Stam (who also designed the chairs). Portrait busts of the nineteenth century founders of an Albany, New York company and two baseball figures (one a tobacco-shop batter and the other a mechanical catcher) are silent company at dinner.

The collector's simply appointed bedroom contains a gilded eagle from the Boston Customs House, a sheet-iron angel weathervane, and a carved ship's figurehead, all made in the eighteenth century. Another prize piece is the weathervane model of Bleriot's plane that once adorned the Poland Spring House in Maine.

the same delicacy of form in a George Ohr pot as in an ancient Sung ceramic vase.

It is the continuing ability to see beyond the period, the maker, or the original use of the object, and to value the unusual or innovative use of materials and forms, that distinguishes Greenspon's collection. That same eye has arranged extremely disparate and unexpected things into a highly individual domestic environment where everything is in formal harmony but where nothing is robbed of its artistic and inventive vitality.

Left: *One corner of the living room contains a rare nineteenth century ship's carving of Daniel Webster and a unique ceramic bust of a black man by P.W. McAdam (1926) found in Ripley, Mississippi. These major folk pieces are flanked by Penitente sculptures from the southwest. Beneath the pedestal (made by the collector) are two mechanical boxers, a diving mask, and a complex automaton from the nineteenth century—pieces which reflect Greenspon's taste for the surrealistic.*

Right: *On a Bauhaus desk the collector has grouped a pre-Columbian mask, a crumpled bowl by the great American potter George Ohr, an optician's device that resembles an African mask, and an American Indian head—part of a ventriloquist's dummy from the Rolling Thunder Indian Medicine Show that toured western New York state.*

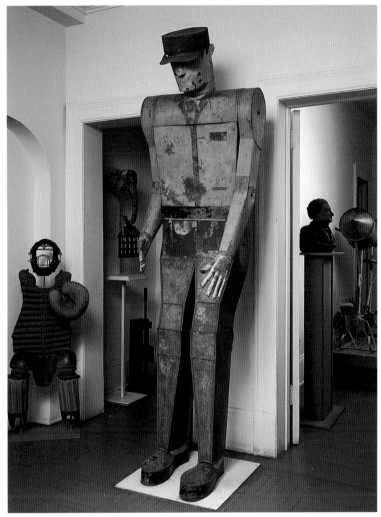

Left: *In the apartment entrance hall, visitors are greeted by a bust of Admiral Dewey, an acorn-capped barber pole, the seat from a 1936 French airplane, the head of an early robot, and a whimsical cow-shaped weathervane.*

Right: *Another corner of the hall holds an old catcher's uniform, a monumental, polychromed metal filling station attendant discovered in Jewett City, Connecticut, and an early American lantern held by an elephant's head.*

18
COLLECTING FOR THE FUTURE

"[Those] who wish to possess objects of art must not only have the means to acquire them but also the skill to choose them—a skill made up of cultivation and judgement, combined with a feeling for their beauty that no amount of study can give, but that study alone can quicken and render profitable." Edith Wharton and Ogden Codman, The Decoration of Houses

Some collections of art are intuitive and sporadic, governed by evolving interests that may change radically over a period of time. A collection of contemporary art may have a regional, national, or even international focus. Only a few collectors have the means or the discipline to create a contemporary collection that is broad in scope and that at once surveys stylistic movements and concentrates on several artists in depth. These sophisticated collectors of contemporary art, who divide their time between New York, Europe, and other parts of the world, are unusually attuned to the international aspects of developments in contemporary art.

The collection featured here, which began as a personal response of a currently New York couple to the art of the late 1960s and the 1970s, has evolved within the last decade into an organized and more systematic program. The purpose of that program is to assemble major works by acknowledged masters of Abstract Expressionism, Color Field painters, minimalists, and in general those artists who emerged in the 1970s and 1980s as significant contributors to cultural history. Nearly seventy-five percent of the works in this collection of over 250 objects deal with recognizable imagery; many others incorporate indirect or latent references to figurative or narrative imagery. Nearly one-half of the ninety American and European artists in the collection are represented by more than one work, and increasing the number of works by others remains one of the goals for the collection. "We want to create a portrait of our time," say the couple.

Very few of the works in this collection have ever been sold off. But as the collection has grown, a great deal of the material has either been put into storage or loaned out to travelling shows and museums. What remains on display in the residences of these collectors has been radically edited. "Art is more powerful if it is allowed to breathe," say the collectors. "We have learned to simplify the rooms, to take things away rather than add them." The New York apartment where some of the collection is installed is elegant in its simplicity and attention to unobtrusive detail. Over the years, window treatments, lighting, and architectural details have all been stripped down and refined. Art dominates the environment, with four simple white sofas grouped in a living room whose splendor comes from paintings and sculpture. A vintage Sam Francis abstraction is hung near a Cy Twombly work from the 1970s. Morris Louis's "Aleph I" (1960) and Robert Motherwell's dramatic abstraction, "Diary of a Painter" (1958), are on opposite walls of the room. A large, vividly colored sculpture by Roy Lichtenstein, called "Double Glass" (1979), and a black lacquer table designed in 1984 by Scott Burton are the sculptural elements in the large, square room, whose fireplace was recently remodeled to include a subtle postmodern mantel.

These collectors consciously try to "create a different ambiance in each room." Changes in color scheme and in the subject matter and texture of the art, combined with a highly sophisticated awareness of how the groupings of pictures and objects intensify one another, accomplish this goal. In the small library, a Dan Flavin neon light sculpture now casts a warm pink glow over paintings by Malcolm Morley, and sculptures by John Chamberlain and Jannis Kounellis. Terra cotta pre-Columbian heads that line the library shelves continue an implicit theme of antique and classical references. In the front hall, a metal floor piece of Carl Andre is echoed by the carefully squared geometry of the recently installed parquet floor. An abstract composition with ravishing, spring-like color by Joan Mitchell is a counterpart to this strict series of grids. The overpowering element in the simply furnished dining room is a diaphanous wall composition by Judy Pfaff. It blossoms across an entire wall and evokes the colors and forms of undersea life. On the opposite wall, a monochromatic "writing" painting by Cy Twombly in grey and white continues a lyrical mode of feeling. There is no random placement in this interior. Objects are consciously categorized "to amplify their formal and associative meaning." A luscious Morris Louis "veil" painting in the bedroom echoes the translucent hues and sensuous folds of a collection of Dale Chihuly's blown glass vases and bowls that have been grouped in a theatrically lighted niche especially constructed for their display. "We've never understood the nervousness about distinguishing between art and craft," say these collectors. "These pieces by Chihuly are such fine examples of the best and most original contemporary glass making. They can be appreciated for what they are: models of excellence in the medium of glass. They do not have to be compared to painting or sculpture."

In the apartment working office, an inlaid, blond, commissioned partner's desk takes up most of the room. On the walls, a pale, textured painting of a riverboat by Joe Zucker, a small work by the Italian painter, Enzo Cucchi, and a beautiful "Teaching Blackboard" by Joseph Beuys embellish the walls without overpowering the space. A small column by Ned Smyth reinforces the idea of texture explored by Zucker's picture.

Surprisingly, this interest in art was originally motivated by a childhood appreciation of eighteenth and nineteenth century European art and architecture, especially the baroque churches and the castles of Ludwig II of Bavaria. The collectors turned to contemporary art collecting as "a unique opportunity to still make mistakes." New art offered the intellectual rigor and visual risk of forming one's own decisions about new material. "Not having a lot of money in the beginning was actually a helpful restriction in that decision-making process," they say.

Courses in aesthetics and art history have honed the skills of the wife in this team, and it was she who was the initial impetus in the collection's formation. Her approach to acquisition is analytical and historical. "I believe in using art history and cultural history to see why a new work has value. When I look at a work of art, I ask what are its influences, its formal concerns? Are the materials provocative? How do they deal with contemporary technology? If it is figurative, I ask, if someone sees it in thirty years, will they care about the narrative, the social, political, or cultural content? I am wary of academicism in art and I believe art must provoke one to deep thought." These collectors have often purchased works by young and unknown artists that may turn out to be "loss leaders." "You can't count on the longevity of any young artist, and no-one can prop up an artist's reputation for long unless the work deserves it." They retain such works as historical footnotes and now tend to try to acquire major pieces which demonstrate a pivotal shift in an artist's development, and to look for works that express an evolution in artistic ideas and materials. "It is important to live with beautiful things," they believe. "If more people could see them, perhaps they would relate more profoundly to a layer of historical content through understanding and experiencing art." That is why the ultimate goal for this collection is to make it available to the public in a place where access to contemporary art is limited. In the meantime, their New York apartment and other homes serve as test sites for the staying power of new art.

Judy Pfaff's ebullient wall composition in the dining room is glimpsed through a living room doorway between paintings by Sam Francis and Morris Louis.

Opposite above: *The simple lines and white upholstry of contemporary furniture complement Cy Twombly's untitled painting, hung asymetrically near the fireplace. The sculpture is Roy Lichtenstein's "Double Glass" from 1979.*

Opposite below: *A blue metal wall sculpture by Donald Judd is complemented by a recently installed, drastically simple window treatment. The Lichtenstein "Double Glass" is in a different position in this later view of the living room.*

Left: *Another view of the living room includes a wall piece by sculptor Lynda Benglis and an exceptional oriental carpet.*

Below: *Robert Motherwell's 1958 "Diary of a Painter" is installed over a postmodern mantel in another view of the living room.*

101

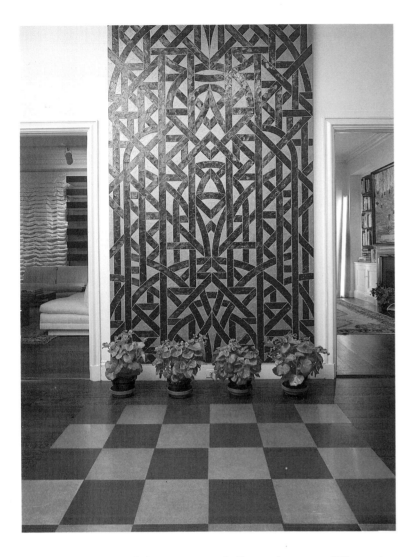

Above: *Two views of the apartment hallway show two different installations: The strong pattern of Valerie Jaudon's painting is very different from the lyrical flourishes of the painting by Joan Mitchell. The Carl Andre floor piece lives equally well with both canvases.*

Opposite top: *In the bedroom, a somber Morris Louis "Veil" painting.*

Opposite bottom: *The serene library is the setting for a recent painting by Malcolm Morley and a group of pre-Columbian terra-cotta sculptures.*

A sculpture by Joel Shapiro inhabits a corner of the living room. Shirred roman shades filter daylight in the early decorative scheme for the living room.

Opposite: *Near the window in an earlier incarnation of the bedroom (than shown on page 102) are a painting by Pat Steir and a polychromed sculpture by Nancy Graves composed of blue Japanese fans and other shapes cast from nature.*

104

19

AN ADVENTUROUS COLLECTION

"Life was enhanced by art." Remy Saisselin

An upper floor of a handsome turn-of-the-century office building in lower Manhattan is home to Hal Bromm. This adventurous art dealer has filled the sunny space (there are windows on all four sides) with an eclectic assortment of recent art and with furniture from many different periods and places. The vivid paintings and sculpture chronicle the stylistic diversity of the last two decades. The bold colors and raw imagery of Rick Prol's recent painting, entitled "Garbage," and the delicate skeins of Mike Bidlo's "Convergence" (his 1983 Jackson Pollock imitation), appear unexpectedly at home with Bromm's Hepplewhite settees and the delicate floral patterns and faded hues of his Aubusson rugs. He has selected his furniture for formal reasons as much as for its materials or historical values. Minimally elegant black-and-white screens from the early 1970s by Rosemarie Castoro provide a perfect foil for sculptor Russell Sharon's brilliant orange, carved, life-sized figures. The high ceilings and generous size of Bromm's yellow salon allow these museum-scale pieces to co-exist comfortably.

Both Castoro and Sharon are artists whom the dealer represents, but Bromm's collecting interests range far beyond the confines of his business. He has always bought work by artists like Robert Longo, Keith Haring, and Julian Opie, whose talent he spotted before they came to the attention of the mainstream. His support has also gone beyond purchasing new work to finding ways to present it publicly. He has always enjoyed introducing such emerging artists to a larger audience, and over the years has mounted "new talent" shows in his two downtown galleries. These have highlighted artists like David Salle, Troy Brauntuch, Robert Yarber, and Ida Applebroog when their work was still largely unrecognized.

In one way or another, Bromm has spent most of his life involved with what he sees as the overlapping and parallel fields of art, architecture, and design. Always intrigued with the arts, he organized theatrical productions as a child and went on to study painting at Pratt Institute in the late 1960s. At Pratt, he says he found himself "becoming a little bored with just making art." An irrepressable Gemini, he decided to expand his knowledge and enrolled in the school's new environmental design program. "It incorporated everything that interested me," he says, "art history, lighting, architecture, interior design, graphics, color science. I realized then that design was really another side of art. I wanted to be an architect, a designer, to present new visual ideas. I also realized I was an entrepreneur."

While still in school Bromm also got a job as a design assistant to Pratt alumna Evelyn Ortner. She and her husband, pioneers in the budding preservation movement in the Park Slope area of Brooklyn, introduced him to the idea of neighborhood renewal. Alerted to the undeveloped potential of many of Manhattan's neglected neighborhoods, Bromm decided that SoHo, already in the early stages of gentrification, was too small and already discovered. Looking further downtown to the wilderness of factory and warehouse buildings south of Canal Street, he became an early resident of what would turn into TriBeCa. In 1973 he moved to 10 Beech Street, opened his own design business, and subsequently bought the building. "All my neighbors were artists, musicians, and other creative people," he says. "There were only a handful of residential buildings then, and at night, when the commercial businesses closed up, it was like a nineteenth century neighborhood." He has continued to be involved in efforts to preserve the special character of TriBeCa and is now Chairman of the Committee for the Washington Market Historic District.

Bromm's professional life and his personal interests have remained inextricably linked since those early TriBeCa days. Becoming an art dealer was a natural outgrowth of those interests; the profession combined the skills of an impresario, the knowledge of how art is made, what it can mean, and how it can change our perception of the environment. "I've always loved introducing new art to people," he says. "I've seen in many different ways how collectors' lives are changed by the art they live with. I feel a bond with the art I own and I've very rarely sold anything." Many of the pieces in his collection are personal—portraits artists he knows have done of him, even Christmas decorations they have made for annual parties.

His strongly developed aesthetic sense is not limited to contemporary art. Like Andy Warhol, his taste is not restricted to a single period, style, or area. The two years that he spent in England after he finished Pratt expanded his existing interest in historic architecture and period furniture and showed him the value of "combining the old and the new." He says that he was struck with the combination of generations of things in English country houses. When he was very young, he was also influenced by trips to country auctions in New Jersey and summer visits to Maine antique stores he made with his parents.

"I like art that pushes me around," he adds. "Some things I used to collect lost interest for me after they became popular." He also has no hierarchies of value in terms of media. "Just

Art dealer Hal Bromm's home reflects both a dedication to contemporary art and an interest in period furniture.

because a ceramic bowl has a different kind of power from a grand Hudson River School painting doesn't mean that the bowl is less intriguing." His home brings together all his interests, and is the setting for his diverse collections of decorative arts, furniture, and art. The overall collection continues to grow and change. It can be seen as a cumulative record of his active life in art and the history of design. His continuing proximity to young artists has given him a particularly adventurous vantage point in the New York art world, and his professional experience as a dealer in new art has made him comfortable taking chances on untried work and discovering artifacts of high quality from the past.

Opposite: A delicately cross-hatched, abstract, free-standing sculpture and an elegant, black-and-white screen by Rosemarie Castoro are both museum-scale works that fit comfortably into the spacious, high-ceilinged salon.

Right: Bromm retained panelling from the offices that once occupied this space and created an unusual study anteroom to his loft bedroom.

Bottom left: A powerful painting of a reaching hand contrasts with the delicacy of an eclectic trio of furniture.

Bottom right: This corner of Bromm's spacious salon features an exotic wall sculpture and Mike Bidlo's 1983 painting, "Convergence," part of the artist's series of Jackson Pollock paintings.

20
UNTRADITIONAL ELEGANCE

"The finest collectors look at their possessions with the feelings of an artist and relive, to some extent, the sensuous and imaginative experiences which lie behind each work." Sir Kenneth Clark

When they were starting out as a young married couple in Zurich, Gilbert and Jacqueline de Botton began to collect Piranesi prints and "English style" furniture. Their subsequent attraction and dedication to contemporary art was motivated both by an interest in the culture of their time and the fact that contemporary art remained relatively inexpensive when compared to art of the past. Realizing that much of the work that fascinated them was coming from America and parts of Europe other than Switzerland, they turned for advice to the young dealer Thomas Amman and for broader education to inveterate collector and dealer Bruno Bischofsberger, whose own holdings encompass everything from contemporary painting to the world's finest collection of modern Scandinavian and Italian glass. Both of these unofficial advisors was unusually well-versed in their knowledge of emerging artists. They were also well connected to the larger art world, a milieu that during the 1970s was becoming increasingly international in scope.

Today the couple divides their time between a London townhouse and a chalet in St. Moritz. The St. Moritz house has become the venue for a collection of the very recent and often challenging painting and sculpture of contemporary American and European artists, complemented by a selective collection of furnishings designed by Italian architect Ettore Sottsass and other members of the Memphis Group who have defined a new and eccentrically colorful variety of furniture design.

Their London townhouse, although built only twenty-five years ago, is in the eighteenth century style. It provides a traditional setting for exceptional collections of modern and contemporary art, rare first editions, and French eighteenth century

The drawing room of this London townhouse is furnished with superb examples of French eighteenth century furniture, including a set of four Louis XVI elmwood armchairs. A portion of Gilbert de Botton's library of rare French bindings occupies the book shelves. Picasso's "Tête d'Homme" (1971), "Nu Allongé" (1971), and "Le Baiser" (1969) display the master's range near the end of his long life.

111

furniture any museum would envy. Jacqueline de Botton declares that contemporary art has "totally mesmerized me." Her dedication to collecting has inevitably led her to devote much of her time to the support of younger British artists and to such institutions as The Royal Academy and the Israel Museum. She is the first non-British trustee of the Royal Academy, and her husband, who is chairman of the Tate Gallery's International Council, is also the first non-British trustee of the Tate. Gilbert de Botton is recognized too as a discriminating and scholarly collector of rare French editions and bindings.

The delicately proportioned rooms of the couple's London residence is unexpectedly small for the display of modern art. Several floors are connected by narrow, winding staircases, and a buttery, blond paint scheme unifies these spaces, as do the pale rugs and the subtle woods used for some of the built-in fittings. The centerpiece in the small front entrance hall is a sinuous sculpture by Naum Gabo that was the artist's model for a much larger sculpture installed in the city of Rotterdam. The de Bottons had the sculpture cleaned after they acquired it and were delighted to find an exquisite combination of metals, colors, and textures underneath the layers of grime. "The cleaning revealed the extraordinary subtlety of the piece," they say. The hall also provides hanging space for a drawing by Brice Marden, a swimming pool painting by David Hockney, a work by the young American artist Jenny Holzer, and a painting by Francis Bacon. Bacon is one of the artists whom the couple has collected in some depth; they now hold a half dozen of his paintings, which include a self-portrait of the artist, a rare portrait of Gilbert de Botton, and a portrait after a life mask of William Blake.

Pablo Picasso is represented in the collection by over fifteen painting and drawings. The de Bottons have installed Picasso's elegiac 1960 version of Manet's *Dejeuner sur l'Herbe* in the dining room on the ground floor. With this major work are also hung R. B. Kitaj's *Aureolin* and a painting on steel by Julian Opie as well as Picasso's powerful *Tête de Femme* from 1971. Other important paintings by Picasso are displayed in the asymmetrical drawing room and the upstairs entrance hall. The de Bottons began acquiring examples of Picasso's late works less than a decade ago when the paintings were still widely considered inferior to his earlier achievements, and were accordingly priced much lower than the works from the artist's more recognized periods of development. Time has proved the strength of the artist's vision at the end of his life and ratified the judgments of these collectors. *Le Baiser* from 1969, *Nu Allonge* from 1971, and *Tête d'Homme*, also painted in 1971, hang in the drawing room as testament to Picasso's artistic powers in old age. It is in the drawing room that Gilbert de Botton also

keeps many of his first editions.

This parlor floor of the house is also where the couple has arranged much of their carefully selected collection of French eighteenth century furniture. The evolution of taste that has informed the couple's art collecting has also developed their preference for these most refined demonstrations of the cabinet maker's skills. Among the pieces they have acquired over the years are a Louis XV table with a serpentine, inlaid top, exquisite marquetry and elegant cabriole legs, a set of four Louis XVI elmwood armchairs, and a Louis XV tulipwood, veneered table stamped by the noted cabinet maker R. V. L. C. Jacqueline de Botton remembers that their initial English style furniture was "most hideous" and says they finally jettisoned it all. The French eighteenth century pieces they have subsequently acquired have been purchased after careful study of the decorative arts of the period and with the help of an expert in the field. The couple has become increasingly discriminating in what pieces they buy, and they now try to find only museum quality examples. Their beautifully shaped and delicately fashioned

Opposite top: *"London Knees," a wry 1966 sculpture of a section of Twiggy's anatomy by Claes Oldenburg, and a Christo drawing of the wrapped Reichstag project are placed in the entrance hall to the library, where three Francis Bacon oil portrait studies are closely hung.*

Opposite bottom: *A curving stairwell is enlivened by an assortment of modern and contemporary painting and sculpture, including "The Pot is Gold," a 1985 wall piece by Anglo-Indian sculptor Anish Kapoor, Jean Tinguely's "Zing-Zing and Co." (a construction that incorporates an electric motor and bell caps), and Kenneth Noland's 1977 shaped canvas, "Regard."*

Below: *Andy Warhol's silkscreen and diamond-dust portrait of Joseph Beuys hangs in Jacqueline de Botton's upstairs office.*

113

furniture, made over two hundred years ago for the aristocratic salons and drawing rooms of pre-revolutionary France, co-exists in surprising harmony with the de Botton's discriminating collection of twentieth century art. "We find it goes with everything," say the collectors.

The de Bottons continue to look at a wide variety of art made by emerging artists and have been particularly supportive of younger British painters and sculptors, as well as their more established and older colleagues. The collection contains nearly a dozen works by David Hockney, sculptures by Stephen Cox, Tony Craigg, Anish Kapoor, Anthony Caro, and Henry Moore. Other British artists represented in the collection are Richard Hamilton, Richard Long, Ian Hamilton Findlay, Frank Auerbach, Gillian Ayers, Lucien Freud, Richard Wentworth, Ben Nicholson, John Latham, and Bill Woodrow.

A painted bronze head by contemporary German artist Marcus Lupertz and drawings by Mario Merz, Christo, Robert Zakanitch, and Joseph Beuys are among the couple's holdings by internationally recognized contemporary artists. The collection also contains works by Scott Burton, Claes Oldenburg, Andy Warhol, Sonia Delaunay, Julian Schnabel, and Arshile Gorky.

The understated elegance of the London house tends to mask the enormous amount of work and thought that has gone into the formation of this collection and its surroundings. "For me, the visual arts are an essential part of life," says Jacqueline de Botton. "Art is different from literature and from music in its continual ability to transform one's daily perceptions. For example, as I constantly look at the Picassos we own I still discover new aspects of the work, new thoughts the artist must have had as he created the paintings." The de Botton collection demonstrates a concentration of imaginative understanding and an intellectual commitment to often difficult or untested art.

21
DISCOVERING A CULTURE

*"Every private collection formed by an individual
in a lifetime is in a way a collection of souvenirs,
a record of travel and discovery."* Jacob Beam

Tom Wheelock's collection of nearly a thousand objects from Burkina Faso represents both a flight from a vocation and the arrival of an unexpected passion. Wheelock had always thought he wanted to be a paleontologist, but in the early 1970s, after he had finished his studies and been offered a job in paleontology at a distinguished institution, he panicked. "I saw myself disappearing into an office and never coming out," he says. His reaction was to turn down the job and to buy a Land Rover. He picked up the vehicle in England, customized it so he could live in it as well as drive it, and started out around the world. After driving across Europe and into Morocco, he left from Algeria to cross the Sahara Desert. His Land Rover attracted a small caravan for the crossing. It included two motorcycles, a dilapidated Citroen van, and a motley group of other vehicles driven by travelers too timid to set out across the great sands on their own. They all got lost, ran into a mine field, ran out of water, but eventually struggled through to Niger. Wheelock proceeded from Niger and found himself in what was then known as Upper Volta, today as Burkina Faso—a small, dry West African nation unfrequented by tourists and inhabited almost entirely by tribal societies. (Upper Volta was colonized by the French in the 1890s.)

Even though "airport art" for tourists now comprises a large part of the export of Burkina Faso, its traditional ritual objects and artifacts have never been widely collected either by Europeans or Americans. Its ornate funerary masks used to be dismissed by collectors as too "decorative." As a result, there are very few examples in Western private collections or museums. And it is only recently that anthropologists have begun to explore and analyze the cultural structures of the area.

To Wheelock the art of Burkina Faso came as a visceral shock. "I had never seen anything like these objects before," he says. "It was a *coup de foudre*. They hit me with an emotional power that was strange and new to me. I hardly understood it, but I knew I had to learn more." The local dealers were "a pack of wolves, and I was a sheep among wolves." It was several months before he actually bought anything.

"I convinced the young American dealer who had first shown me the objects to introduce me to one of his native runners. I gave the runner $200 and asked him to bring me about twenty old objects. He was gone into the bush for a month. The first things be brought me looked odd—too new. Then, as he began to bring in older pieces that seemed more authentic, I was confronted one morning by the local constable. I was accused of stealing the pieces! I ended up in the local court. The major dealers in town were the source of the complaint and were there in the court room. I discovered that my runner had been 'borrowing' pieces from these dealers and bringing them to me. I settled things by returning everything. An alarming experience, but a terrific way to begin an education!"

This was how Wheelock met the better dealers in town, who then became his primary sources of objects. They also taught him indirectly how to recognize the best works. "Nobody would ever show you the good pieces till the last. They usually kept them under the bed. I learned what price to pay by letting pieces pass. Things I didn't buy still haunt me, but they just seemed too expensive at the time."

Months passed, and Wheelock had himself a load of African art stored in a shed. He began to ship the elaborately carved and polychromed masks and slender, anthropomorphic flutes, fertility dolls, even a carved door, back to America in crates the size of couches that he built and packed himself. His first stay in the West African country had by then stretched to nearly two years. He never did make it the rest of the way around the world.

Selling the Land Rover to a missionary for as much as he had paid for it, Wheelock returned to New York in 1974. But his collecting had only begun. Over the next several years he returned to Burkina Faso two or three times a year on trips that lasted for as long as a month and a half. Each trip added to the collection. "I bought in bulk, but it never made prices different. During those years I often sold objects I winnowed out at the less prestigious branch of the Parke-Bernet auction house—to support my habit—but I was very careful not to sell anything I really liked." Trying to learn more about the culture whose objects so fascinated him, and about the nature and meaning of the objects themselves, Wheelock could find little written documentation. "There was no literature to turn to." He even travelled through European ethnographic museums searching for other examples of the work, and photographed and catalogued what little he discovered. "Nobody in this country was very interested in art from Burkina Faso," he recalls. "Susan Vogel, then a curator at the Metropolitan Museum, would come over and look every time I got a new shipment."

Wheelock's consuming interest in this concentrated area of

Funerary masks that mimic spirits, animals, and butterflies, some sacred ancestor figures, and carved bobbins from the region inhabit the collector's living room and surround a drawing by Hans Hartung hung on a mirrored wall above the fireplace.

Opposite: *Another group of animal masks—highly sacred objects in their culture of origin—are boldly carved and painted. They retain the raffia which covers the heads of the men who wear them in tribal funerary dances.*

Above: *A stylized butterfly mask is installed in Wheelock's traditionally furnished dining room.*

Left: *Symbols painted on these tribal masks usually represent myths of origin. The brilliant black, red, and white animal spirit mask in the collector's hallway is hung near female ancestor figures and a modern sculpture by Texas artist Michael Tracy. Grass paper makes a suitable background for the works of art.*

Right: *A polychromed Bwa mask from Burkina Faso.*

119

African art has ended up re-shaping his life. After Susan Vogel became the director of the Center for African Art in Manhattan, the collector's volunteer efforts on the part of the museum gradually developed into a full-time job. He no longer makes his African journey, and the pace of his collecting has slowed down markedly since 1978. Objects are now much more expensive and difficult to locate, so Tom Wheelock and his wife Mary Jane, a free–lance curator and art appraiser, are content mainly to live with the existing collection in their New York apartment, using the maid's room as storage space for objects they rotate in and out of view.

In the course of his collecting, Wheelock had tried to avoid objects that would need extensive restoration, and he has little trouble in maintaining the pieces he has. "The biggest concern is the raffia on the masks," he says. "It tends to disintegrate over time, and there is no good way to preserve it."

Perhaps the most illuminating adjunct to this collection for an outsider is the videotape Wheelock shows of the actual funerary dances and other ceremonies in Burkina Faso. Made over the past five years by an American art historian, the tape cap-tures the unearthly whirling, stamping, and gliding of ritual celebration, transformed by the elaborate, theatrical masks and headdresses into buffalo, warthogs, antelopes—all fierce and protective spirits. A member of the Bwa tribe delicately careens in a huge butterfly mask. His dancing brings to life a similar butterfly mask that occupies Wheelock's living room wall. The tape records ceremonies and costumes which will almost certainly be lost to Europeanized members of the tribe's future generations, for no man who wears western clothes is allowed to learn the solemn and secret intricacies of these traditions.

To see the tape is to realize how little of such a culture can be understood from the inert objects themselves, no matter how powerful their aura as works of art. Wheelock is keenly aware of such cultural contradictions, and of the pitfalls in merely taking this art out of its context without direct experience of that context. But as the traditional ceremonies wither away, and as the traditional jewelry, locks, doors are being replaced by plastic, metal, and modern hardware, he is glad to have preserved what bits of this animist culture he has been able to acquire . . . and display in a New York apartment.

A spare maid's room has become the storage space for many of the objects in this large, highly specialized collection of West African art.

22
A TWENTIETH CENTURY CLASSIC

"It is not only the person . . . who puts his thought on canvas with a brush, who is an artist . . . The vehicle of expression does not matter. It is the spirit that counts. The woman who arranges a room charmingly . . . the man who binds a book in good taste . . . or lays out a garden that gives delight—all are artists in their way." John Wanamaker

What has fascinated this New York businessman are the photography and decorative arts of the first half of this century. For over a decade he has made his apartment a distinctive repository of fine and wittily related pieces. The key to his collection and its arrangement is his strict adherence to an idea of formal quality, whether represented by a delicately geometric Frank Lloyd Wright standing lamp, an unusual 1926 metal side table constructed with fan-shaped leaves by the little-known European designer Pierre Chareau, or Charles Sheeler's photograph of factory smokestacks and walkways.

The constructivist and precisionist photographs that appear throughout the apartment—some hung in groups, others propped next to arangements of industrial objects on a Jean Michel Frank table from the 1930s—were until recently uncelebrated. A penetrating eye for elegance, for strength of subject matter and composition, formed the photographic part of the collection long before the photographers themselves were widely known or their work had become pricey.

The collector's continuing interest in what might be called the machine aesthetic embraced both the decorative and industrial products of the time, lending them a resonance as fascinating as that of the photographic works. So Walter Darwin Teague's design for the Kodak Bantam camera, mass produced in 1944, has become transformed into an art object, as has the enamelled thermos bottle that Henry Dreyfuss designed in the mid-1930s. What this collection exemplifies is the way someone with a highly developed sensitivity to the sculptural properties inherent in objects can see the "art" in them, and the relationships between them. Having the instincts of a detective becomes a necessity in the formation of such a collection. In many cases, one must acquire the object before knowing exactly

One of this collector's more remarkable acquisitions is this lustrous panel by Jean Dupas for the ocean liner S.S. Normandie. It was found languishing in a junk shop. Other known panels are in the Metropolitan Museum.

121

who made or designed it, and then spend time tracking down the information through old magazines, catalogues, and files. One such acquisition here is the lustrous panel over the mantel—painted by Jean Dupas for the fabulous and tragic ocean liner, the S.S. *Normandie*—which was found languishing in a junk shop. All other known panels are in the Metropolitan Museum!

The idea of modernism takes on an added dimension when expressed so clearly through decorative and utilitarian objects. It is as if the collector were filling in pieces of a large and elegant puzzle, a puzzle that is not only beautiful but also highly informative about the nature of our time.

Below and opposite left: *Two expressions of this apartment's theme of formal arrangement: A grouping of industrial objects on a Jean Michel Frank table from the 1930s aligned with a disparate but harmonious cluster of photographs, and a delicately geometric Frank Lloyd Wright standing lamp.*

Top right: *A 1926 metal side table constructed with fan-shaped leaves by the European designer Pierre Chareau.*

Bottom right: *A Marcel Breuer table with a Gilbert Rhode clock holds a 1920 French art-deco cigarette case, a photograph by Charles Sheeler—one of the foremost precisionist artists of the 1930s—a 1928 table lamp by Wilhelm Wagenfeld, and a 1914 silver serving tray by Kalo.*

23
"YOU LEARN FROM LIVING WITH THE ART"

"It takes a trained eye, a special sensibility and love to recognize that essential 'quality' which constitutes greatness in any form of artistic creation." Douglas Cooper

Collecting art came naturally to Agnes Gund. While growing up in the mid-West she was deeply influenced by the quality and scholarship she saw evidenced at the Cleveland Museum of Art under director William Milliken and Sherman Lee who followed Milliken in the director's post.

Both men were also long-time friends of her family. Her parents had always collected Western paintings and Spanish art. In high school, her art history teacher, Sarah McClennan, encouraged her museum going, and when Gund was still in college she started buying contemporary prints herself.

Two other women collectors were to become decisive influences in her motivation to collect and in her ongoing art education. In Cleveland, Katherine White's great respect and love for art served as both catalyst and example. Mrs. White subsequently would leave her important collection of African art to the Seattle Art Museum. Says Gund about the woman she deeply admired, "She was very serious about scholarship and learning." On the East Coast, Emily Tremaine took a fancy to the young collector and became a kind of art-world mentor to her. "She took me around to galleries and to artists' studios from the early sixties on. And from Emily Tremaine I learned always to look for authenticity of feeling in a work of art. All her things were so beautiful, it was almost impossible to distinguish one's favorite among them."

One of the studios the two women visited was that of the painter Mark Rothko on East 69th Street in New York City. Agnes Gund, who greatly admired a magnificent yellow Rothko belonging to the Tremaines, bought her own green and magenta Rothko painting directly from the artist as a result of that visit. This initial introduction to Rothko then led to subsequent meetings and a meaningful friendship before the painter died.

The Tremaines also owned Jasper Johns' dazzling "White Flag." "It really was the masterpiece of the collection," Agnes Gund recalls. "Having known and loved that painting made me feel lucky to be able to buy the Johns map painting which now hangs in the apartment dining room. It was also when I was with Emily that I bought Neil Jenney's 'Dog and Cat,' right from the studio fifteen years ago. At that point Jenney's work was very little known and was considered difficult."

When Agnes Gund and her family moved from Shaker Heights, Ohio, to Greenwich, Connecticut, in 1972, the focus of her collecting shifted. "While the children were growing up in Greenwich, I got very interested in sculpture." An early commission went to Claes Oldenburg for his monumental sculpture, "The Mitt," a 12-foot-high, first-baseman's mitt made of Corten steel, lead, and cypress wood. A photograph of the witty piece is in the library; the sculpture itself is now on loan to Wave Hill in Riverdale, New York. During those years the family also secured a site in Greenwich for Mary Miss's sunken well project, which the artist had received a National Endowment for the Arts fellowship to execute. Increasingly Agnes Gund found herself drawn to other environmental sculpture projects and became involved in helping artists facilitate such work. "This

Opposite: *Bradley Walker Tomlin's abstract canvas "Final Painting, #15" is installed over an antique side table in the dining room. The dining room table and chairs were designed by Gwen-lin Loo and the candlesticks by sculptor Bryan Hunt.*

Above: *Gaudi's elaborate gilded frame surrounds a simple mirror over the living room fireplace. Nearby, a painting by Mark Rothko, and beyond, Frank Stella's 1963 "Plant City." The glass coffee table holds a sculpture by Tony Smith and a ceramic pitcher by Andrew Lord.*

led to being on museum committees, art juries, and to an involvement with Art Outreach." One of these projects was "Studio in the Schools," a program designed to bring working artists into New York City's public school classrooms. This highly successful program, begun by the collector, and by Pat Hewitt, at that time director of Joint Foundation Support, also Georgie Alexander Greene, who ran the New York City school system's art program, has been in operation for eleven years. Gund prizes the two boxes of children's drawings she was given in recognition for her work with the pioneering program—eloquent evidence of what contact with artists has meant to many New York school children.

During the 1970s, Agnes Gund also went back to Harvard to get a master's degree in art history. The courses she took there taught her that "an emotional attachment to art does not impede one's judgement; in fact, it deepens it." Her studies also opened her eyes to the attractions of drawings. "Now I really collect drawings, and I would like to have even earlier works than what I have been able to get." Among the drawings that fill the walls of a long, white hallway in her Manhattan apartment are works by Picasso, Frantisek Kupka, Myron Stout, Francesco Clemente, Ellsworth Kelly, and Christo. It is an assortment that reflects an appreciation of nuance and subtle line.

While the children have been known to complain that the house looks too much like a museum, the apartment in fact exemplifies how one can combine a magnificent collection of contemporary works with a very comfortable and informal environment. It is a place that clearly is lived in, not one simply given over to display without thought for comfort or the differing needs and desires of an active family. It has evolved to meet those needs. The dark brown library walls are the unexpected site for a Sol LeWitt circular wall piece and display various personal art-world memorabilia—letters, sketches, photographs—and a selection of pre-Columbian and African sculptures. One of the prize pieces here is a beautiful and ancient Chinese bronze vessel that belongs to her husband. A Gerrit Rietveld chair and a small, geometric table of black ebony designed by Scott Burton are highly sculptural elements in the room.

The Johns painting, "Between the Clock and the Bed," and a large, multi-panelled painting of flowers by Pat Steir dominate a living room full of inviting sofas. A mirror with a heavy, sinuous, gilded frame designed by the visionary Spanish architect, Antoní Gaudí, is at once a beautiful object and a powerful decorative addition to the spacious and comfortable room. A large, blown-glass shell by mastercraftsman Dale Chihuly, a ceramic pitcher by Andrew Lord, and other contemporary ceramics by Betty Woodman reflect the collector's interest in contemporary decorative arts that are bold in both form and color. The presence of sculpture is ubiquitous but not intrusive in the apartment. The dining room holds a large, horizontal "Reclining Woman," one of Mary Frank's monumental terra cotta pieces,

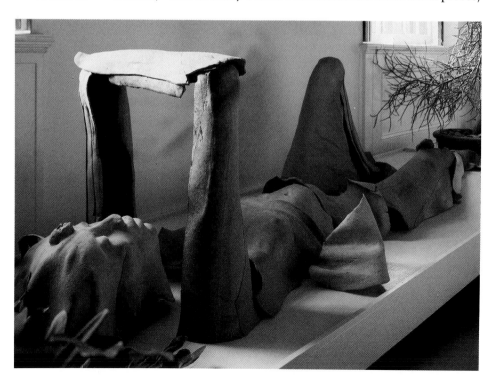

Mary Frank's monumental terra-cotta "Woman" rests beneath the dining room windows.

126

and another figurative bronze sculpture by Judy Shea, placed on the floor. In the living room, a small piece by Tony Smith rests on the simple glass coffee table and a Carl Andre made of large, raw wood beams stands beside the sofa. Over the doorway to the dining room a delicate airship made by Bryan Hunt soars unobtrusively. Agnes Gund's active interest in sculpture as well as painting makes her an unusual collector: very often it is difficult for people to perceive both mediums with an equal ability to distinguish quality.

Most of her paintings—including an important, early Frank Stella star-shaped painting, "Masterpiece," a major Roy Lichtenstein from the early 1960s, a Willem de Kooning, a Bradley Walker Tomlin, a delectable Hans Hofmann, works by Dorothea Rockburne, a handsome, early Larry Rivers, a Robert Rauschenberg, the magenta Rothko, and a new picture by the young artist Mark Tansey, as well as a recent Sandro Chia—were acquired in what she calls "spurts of collecting." While her work as a member of the acquisitions committee at the Museum of Modern Art and her constant attendance at galleries have kept her "looking at new art," the high prices and critical hyperbole surrounding much recent work has disappointed her, as has what she perceives to be a lack of craftsmanship in the work of many of the more ostentatiously promoted new artists.

She has often passed up works by important artists. "I now won't buy certain things that I do think are major because the art is too fugitive, too fragile." Although she has bought several pieces—usually in varying media—by artists she continues to admire (among them Louise Bourgeois, Frank Stella, Arshile Gorky), she says she sometimes wishes she had collected in greater depth. She also continues to be fascinated by sculpture, though owning more major pieces is prohibited simply by limitations of space in the apartment.

Agnes Gund is a collector who recognizes that collecting entails a responsibility not only to the art she owns but even more to the preservation and dissemination of culture. Her own commitment to art, extended well beyond the objects themselves, has fostered a continuing relationship with museums and educational institutions. She is generous with gifts and long-term loans of works of art. She is also careful to determine that the works she gives or loans go to places where "they will really do the most good in the collection."

Her own collection contains an unusual number of works by women artists, including drawings and other works on paper, ceramics, and furniture. The glass-and-steel dining room tables and chairs are commissioned works from the talented artist and designer Gwen-lin Goo.

Rarely has Agnes Gund bought at auction, and she has sold only three or four of her artworks during all the years she has been acquiring art. She is more likely to give things to institutions. "You learn from living with the art," she says. "When art is around you all the time, you just can't help developing a good eye."

Pat Steir's large multi-panelled painting of flowers commands one corner of the living room.

Above: *"Dutch Masters" by Larry Rivers was painted in 1963, and Roy Lichtenstein's Pop Art painting from 1962 is ironically entitled "Masterpiece."*

Opposite: *Over the living room sofa, Jasper Johns's "Between the Clock and the Bed," an encaustic painting done in 1981; below, in the foreground Carl Andre's massive 1975 sculpture made of raw wooden beams entitled "The Way North, East, South and West.*

24
TRANSFORMING THE MUNDANE

"Style was what you bought at the store; taste was how you put it together." William Seale

Izhar Patkin's loft on the Lower East Side of Manhattan is his studio and office as well as his home. This young Israeli-born, now American artist is a wizard at transforming the commonplace into the unexpectedly witty or magical. He finds the affinities between very dissimilar things, including the treasures hidden in the trashy, and creates an unmistakably personal milieu from the most disparate colors, objects, materials, and works of art. And using his knowledge of stenciling, tiling, and construction, he has done most of the work himself.

"The way I built this loft," he says, "was to start from two basic premises. When I got it the space was raw and completely open, so the first idea was to install the false columns to define space." With the curtains that fit inside the pillars drawn, individual rooms are created. When they are pulled back, the space flows together. They are the flexible dividers, the movable walls. "Before this," Patkin recalls, "I lived in a loft that was completely open. It didn't work for me. I always felt as if there were nowhere else to go."

His second idea was that "white was not the ground color." The main room—a combination of front hall, living room, and dining room—is used to display a changing group of paintings, sculptures, and found objects. "This is where I'll bring a painting I'm working on and see how it holds up. I like to look at them while I'm eating." The artist took the red and yellow walls of his middle room from the colors of a Buddhist temple. "I've always noticed that things which look cheesy in one culture are sacred in another. I think of borrowing such things, of making such unexpected juxtapositions, as a way to add value, add joy. I think that ideas about what is valuable are usually artificial. Anyone can invest value in an object someone else might consider worthless. Every person creates their own story. The way this loft is—that's part of my story. It's a cross between a Buddhist temple and a Spanish bodega."

Such transpositions and transformations are colored by Patkin's subtle humor. There is wit in his stenciled floor of a silhouetted rooster and a checkerboard pattern lifted from traditional New England designs and in his use of a T-shirt with a *faux* Lichtenstein image as an antimacassar on the back of a kitchen chair.

He has Kim MacConnel's painted desk and chair because of their layering of visual meaning as much as for their bold color and pattern.

"Collectors don't really have the flexibility I have. I create my own environment, using the works of my friends and my own work. It's constantly changeable. Here it's not a big deal to hammer another nail into the wall and rehang things, or to take down fabric and staple it another way. In Israel I would never do that. There you must revere even a wall because of its status as a historical relic."

A blue papier-mache rock rescued from a stage set by artist Judy Pfaff sits on the floor next to a collie dog sculpture by Keilly Jenkins in a somewhat surreal companionship with some of Patkin's own modelled wax heads and torsos. Pasted up on one of the pillars is a Barbara Kruger poster, its message in German. "It really seemed like propaganda [in German]" says Patkin, "and up like that it looks purer than if it were blown up and framed in aluminum and glass."

He has fashioned a dining room out of fabrics, a staple gun, and some elaborately made shades of clear plastic and colored ribbons and cellophane. High on the windowed front wall is a paperbag frieze by Thomas Lanigan-Schmidt, turned into a tipsy row of miniature tenements. At night the piece lights up, becoming the chandelier.

"It all has to have wit," Patkin stresses, "and the rooms give clues about my work to anyone who comes in and cares to notice them. This loft is my laboratory."

Opposite top: The artist had a recycled armchair upholstered in white naugahyde and uses a **faux**-*Lichtenstein t-shirt he bought from a street vendor as an antimacassar; the life-size sculpture of Lassie is by Keilly Jenkins. Beside the maintenance-free pet is a blue papier-maché rock made as part of the set for a dance performance by Judy Pfaff. On the walls, paintings by William Wegman, Ehry Anderson, Richard Phillip, and Patkin himself. The wax sculptures are also Patkin's creations.*

Opposite bottom: Closed plaid-and-striped curtains, made by the artist, create moveable walls in what was an open loft. The paintings are by Patkin and his artist friends. An ordinary kitchen table has been transformed into an elegant banquette with a table cover of green velvet and red-and-green fringe that parodies some pretentions of decorating. The large painting is "Death Boat," a recent work made of painted silk on metal by James Naires.

130

Deine
Freudensmomente
haben die
Präzision
militärischer Strategie

Opposite: *Izhar Patkin's "living" room is a riot of contrasting pattern and color that joyfully disdains conventional good taste. The fringed table cloth is by Patkin, as are the decorated pinball machine (lower right) and the stenciled floor. Furniture is by Kim MacConnel and Doreen Gallo. The black-and-white poster, whose message in German says "Your moments of joy have the precision of a military strategy," is by Barbara Kruger.*

Below: *This view of Patkin's dining room demonstrates his imaginative and boldly designed transparent plastic shades, which simultaneously obscure a tenement view and admit available light. A zany vase by Kim MacConnel is both a collage of found objects and a centerpiece. Over the window valance, the paper-bag frieze of miniature tenement buildings by Thomas Lanigan-Schmidt lights up at night.*

133

Patkin's bedroom does double duty as his office. He links together an Arts and Crafts desk and bed to form his "control center". On the massive desk, a Peruvian wire mask and a fanciful epergne by Robert Kushner contrast with a folk art Mexican rooster. The epergne and the rooster reappear in close-up against Patkin's black painting, "Sitting Angel."

25
A LIFELONG EDUCATION OF THE SENSES

*"To collect the art of one's own time is to define
the tradition of the future." Gene Baro*

Now in her eighties, Lydia Winston Malbin may be said to have grown up with the twentieth century. More than forty years after she and her late first husband, the lawyer Harry Winston, began acquiring art in Detroit, Michigan, this collection stands today as one of the most significant private collections of futurist art and the movement's ancillary documents. It is also rich with works from most of the major movements in twentieth century art, containing examples of cubist, Fauve, de Stijl, Dada, surrealist, constuctivist, abstract expressionist, color field and minimalist painting. Also part of the collection are sculpture, prints, drawings, sketchbooks, illustrated books and supporting documents which all demonstrate (often in considerable depth) a particular artist's thought processes in different media. Time has more than ratified the taste and judgment which formed this collection—one any museum would envy—and it now appears as a virtual visual history of modern art in general and of futurism in particular. But when Lydia Malbin began to collect seriously in the years after World War II, she was buying art that was largely unknown, untried, or ignored.

"I started to do this to educate myself," says Mrs. Malbin, who now lives with her collection in a light-filled modern apartment in Manhattan furnished with elegant and understated Scandinavian modern pieces from the 1950s and early 1960s. Far smaller than her former Detroit residence, the apartment is crammed with art, and every closet seems a repository for supporting documents, catalogues, and files for a collector who also possesses the inquisitive soul of an historian and the scrupulous methodology of a curator and a registrar combined.

"People in Detroit thought I was quite mad when we started collecting modern art so long ago," she remembers. "It was all too new." As the daughter of the noted architect Albert Kahn, who himself was a collector of Impressionist and other late nineteenth century art, Mrs. Malbin was already comfortable with original works of art when she and her husband began to acquire pictures by Marc Chagall, Lyonel Feininger, Chaim Soutine, Maurice de Vlaminck, and the American artist John

Marin that marked the beginning of the collection. Her father's wooden T–square hangs in her library, and she has a Monet from his collection in her bedroom. Her own education at Cranbrook and her studies in ceramics there brought her into contact with designers, craftsmen, and artists who were her peers and familiarized her with the seminal ideas of modernism.

Her education must also have helped to form her particular interest in understanding how an individual artist works in different media. "I have been fascinated with how a given artist will express himself in various materials, and not only in painting or sculpture," she stresses. Thus her enthusiastic acquisition of ceramics by Picasso and of a striking, blue-and-white area rug designed by the artist and made in Paris in the late 1950s, as well as his 1921 synthetic cubist painting, "Still Life with Guitar."

Expanding beyond what Detroit had to offer, Mrs. Malbin began travelling with her husband and often with her children—first to New York and subsequently to Europe—as collecting art became an increasingly serious pursuit. "At that time, there were very few dealers showing what I was interested in. But those who did exist were important collaborators in our education, always ready to teach us about what was going on." Such New York dealers as Kurt Vallentin, Karl Nierendorf, Pierre Matisse, Alfred Steiglitz, and Rose Fried became friends as well as suppliers of pictures. They were among the handful of art dealers who showed and sold contemporary art in America during the 1940s and early 1950s. Mrs. Malbin also patronized Peggy Guggenheim's Art of This Century Gallery and says she was one of the first private collectors ever to buy a Jackson Pollock. "I have rarely bought a work of art on first sight," she says, "but one day in 1946 I walked into Peggy Guggenheim's gallery and saw this painting by an unknown artist called Jackson Pollock. I bought it on the spot." The easel–sized picture, dense with skeins of dark colors, still hangs in her hallway. Reflecting on the proliferation of galleries, art–related publications, museums devoted to modern and contemporary art, and the fleets of collectors who currently troll the art world for new work, Mrs. Malbin sees a different environment from the one she so assiduously explored. "There was no one to compete with when I started collecting," she recalls. "And art didn't represent checks."

Her need to educate herself led her not only to the study of the then slim body of written material on modern art but also to further travel and ultimately to the artists themselves. The Winstons were introduced to futurist art (largely overlooked in America, the movement itself had come to a close with the advent of World War I, and by the 1940s many of its most important members were already dead) through Gino Severini with

Umberto Boccioni's "Unique Forms of Continuity in Space," a seminal futurist sculpture, is grouped with other sculptures by Jean Arp and Constantin Brancusi. The stunning view from Mrs. Malbin's living room across Central Park is a fortuitous acquisition of what the Japanese call "borrowed scenery."

136

whom they became friends during one of their European trips. He was one of the key artist survivors of this radical art movement. Although the artist had forsaken the futurist style and moved on, his influence led them both to his early works and to the works of F. T. Marinetti, Giacomo Balla, Umberto Boccioni, Mario Sironi, and Luigi Russolo, as well as to their surviving relatives. Often it was from the families of those futurist painters that the collectors acquired not only sculpture and paintings but also letters, notebooks, drawings, and other documents that give the collection its unique historical texture. From Boccioni's sister Mrs. Malbin got many of her over 250 Boccioni drawings. She also owns the artist's palette. "The way I found things and the people I met have added authenticity to the collection," she feels. Her passion for futurism also led her back to an interest in the rare works by the sculptor Medardo Rosso, and she was able to acquire four of his fragile wax sculptures.

The collection also includes important works by other European and American artists who were architects of modern art. Cubist works by Georges Braque, Picasso, Metzinger and Juan Gris; paintings by Robert Dalauney, Auguste Herbin, Piet Mondrian, Max Ernst, Joan Miró, and Kurt Schwitters are amplified in meaning by the presence of sculpture by Hans Arp, Naum Gabo and Gaston Lachaise. There are contemporary works by Kenneth Noland, Paul Feeley, Morris Louis, and Frank Stella, whose debts to cubism and constructivism are made apparent by the company of their elder artists.

As involvement with the ideas and the works of all these twentieth century artists grew, Mrs. Malbin says she began to feel the need to educate others beyond herself and her family about the art. Collecting led her to work with museums and universities. "I've been very active with museums," she says. She was acting commissioner of art in Detroit, an honorary curator at the Detroit Institute of the Arts, and is a member of the twentieth century art committee at the Metropolitan Museum of Art as well as of the art committees at Vassar College and Bennington College. Selections from the collection have often been loaned to exhibitions and were the subject of major shows at the Detroit Institute of Arts, Yale University, and the Guggenheim Museum. She has also opened her home to students in art history, who have been allowed to use the entire collection as a study center. Many a young dealer, curator, or historian recalls the thrill of handling original materials for the first time thanks to Mrs. Malbin, who over the years has always acted as the collection's curator and record-keeper. Her comprehensive files contain individual records for each work of art and comprise an important historical record in their own right. "I take all the responsibility for my own opinions and choices,"

Above: *In the library, the T-Square of Mrs. Malbin's father, the architect Alfred Kahn, hangs with works by Andy Warhol, Georges Braque, and Auguste Herbin. To the left, Giacomo Balla's 1918 masterpiece, "The Injection of Futurism," has been placed above an antique cabinet that holds a group of sculptures and ceramics.*

Opposite: *The halls of the apartment are completely filled with works from Mrs. Malbin's collection. The kitchen beyond also contains many posters and paintings.*

139

she says. "But I've learned from dealers who wanted to teach and I've only gone to the best sources. So many people helped me to learn that I have felt it imperative to help others in turn."

Mrs. Malbin's own historian's understanding of modern art has also clearly made her sensitive to the ideas of modern design that paralleled its development. She has never traded or sold any of her works of art. She says she has only once bought at auction, getting two drawings by Alexander Archipenko. Her perception of other media extends to the decorative arts, and her furniture has a strong and enduring character in its own right. As she wrote in an essay, "Collecting Modern Art," composed as part of the catalogue of a travelling show of works selected from her collection, "On every occasion, we have been honest in our preferences, and this makes for coherence and unity. . . . Quality counts above all else. The charming, the pretty, the decorative, the too appealing and popular, we do not trust. A work of lasting interest must go far beyond this." She cautions: "For the dedicated collector, the understanding of art must be a constant and continuing process of observing. . . . The education of the eye never ceases."

Opposite top: *Along the left wall of the apartment living room hang Picasso's synthetic cubist "Still Life with Guitar" from 1921, "The Brothers Fratellini," a 1927 painting by Miro, and Brancusi's magnificent bronze "Head of a Negress." These important works of twentieth century art are complemented by a classic Scandinavian modern sofa, occasional tables and chairs of fifties design, and a brilliant blue-and-white area rug by Picasso.*

Opposite bottom: *On another wall of the living room hangs a selection of Mrs. Malbin's early-twentieth century masterpieces, including Boccioni's painting, "Street Pavers" (far left), Severini's 1913 painting, "Dancers Beside the Sea" (center), and Robert Delaunay's "Still Life with Red Tablecloth" (1937) at the far right. A cherished piecrust table is one of Mrs. Malbin's few antiques.*

Above: *One corner of the apartment living room contains (from right to left) an early painting by Fernand Lèger, Giacomo Balla's "Stairway of Farewells," Morris Louis's 1959 work, "Quo Numine Lasso," and in the hall beyond, one of his stripe paintings from 1962, "Late Flowering."*

141

26
A FLAIR FOR REFINEMENT

*"I do not understand painters who do not collect
. . . The urge to collect is part of the urge to create
art." William Copley*

There is no junk in Nabil Nahas's beautiful downtown New York loft. This painter of meditative, elegantly monochromatic abstractions has refined his environment to reflect a discriminating interest in art and design, one that spans different cultures and centuries. His own artistic career, like that of Arshile Gorky, an artist he deeply admires, has taken him from the Middle East and Europe to America. His furniture, ceramics, textiles, and collection of paintings and sculpture demonstrate an understanding of art that is unusually cosmopolitan in taste and particularly startling to find in lower Manhattan.

A suite of twenty-two pieces of gilded furniture made for Compiègne in 1809 by Jacob Des Malter dominates the open sweep of the loft. It is arranged in strategic groupings, and is complemented by other furniture from the 1920s and 1930s by Jean Michel Frank. The loft also holds a vast French Empire bed, a Wassily chair, some unrefinished French tole tables, and several carved Senufo laundry benches that serve as portable stools. The interior was recently rebuilt to better house Nahas's collection and to provide more space for the objects and for living needs. Nahas now paints in a separate studio. When he acquired his suite of Des Malter chairs and sofas, he was afraid that the massive, gilded wood furniture "might be too pompous." It has turned out to be both comfortable and in harmony with everything else. In the renovation and refinement process, he slowly bought what interested him, "giving away things as I got tired of them. A while ago I put a lot of Eames and Nelson furniture 'on extended loan.' "

Oriental carpets, laid over wall-to-wall sisal rugs, reflect an interest Nahas has pursued since college days. "I find rugs in small antique shops everywhere. I learned about them first when I had a summer job with the great rug dealer Voitech, and I've collected them ever since."

Nahas grew up in Egypt and Lebanon, was educated in America, and has been deeply influenced by French and European culture. He surrounds himself with art and objects that speak to him visually. His taste for twentieth century French and

Italian painting and for French ceramics from the 1920s reflects a love of gesture and surface modulation. These qualities are repeatedly transmuted in his own paintings. His visual library includes paintings and drawings by André Masson, Lucio Fontana, Henri Michaux, Arshile Gorky, Jean Dubuffet, Jean Fautrier, and Auguste Herbin. He has often been able to acquire works by the artists when they were unfashionable. "I still buy the works of artists I liked as a kid. The first drawing I bought when I was sixteen was a Michaux," says Nahas. "I always seem to look at what very few others are paying attention to."

The highlight of the artist's ceramics collection is his group of exquisite planters and vases by Raoul Dufy, bought in Paris at a time when hardly anyone recognized Dufy's ceramic gifts. "Park Avenue collectors too often buy what they are told to

buy," says Nahas, "but if you have developed your eye, you can see for yourself what is fine." He also may sell something in order to acquire something else, and has found that auctions can be a source for overlooked works. "When I bought the Gorky, no-one was focussing on it at the auction." His late Maurice Denis painting and drawing were acquired directly from the daughter of the artist. He also owns pieces by the contemporary painter Al Held, with whom he studied at Yale, and a delicate cut-out by Alex Katz, his friend since Nahas moved to New York in 1973.

Knowledge and sophisticated taste are the basis of this very selective combination of the fine and the decorative arts, as is an artistic sensibility that is never afraid to go against the grain of fashion to acquire the unexpected and the uncommon thing.

Opposite: *A drawing by Henri Michaux hangs above the fragment of a seventeenth century marble figure.*

Below: *A shelf beneath the loft windows holds a cut-out portrait of Ada by American artist Alex Katz and several Semitic antiquities and African pieces. To the right of the windows are hung two of Arnaldo Pomodoro's slashed and punctured paintings.*

Opposite top and top left: *A suite of furniture made for the palace at Compiègne in 1809 by Jacob Des Malter sumptuously furnishes Nahas's New York loft. The artist has combined the massive French chairs and sofas with pieces by Jean Michel Frank, African objects that serve as low stools, and several small unrefinished French toleware tables. One of the artist's large abstract paintings is installed at the far end.*

Bottom left: *A small painting by Dubuffet rests on top of a cupboard that holds some of the artist's collection of early twentieth century French ceramics, and a large canvas by Henri Michaux is installed on the wall to the left.*

Opposite, bottom left: *A small painting by Chaim Soutine is installed on an easel next to the massive Empire sofa.*

Opposite, bottom right: *Two ceramic lamp bases painted by Raoul Dufy in the 1920s are from Nahas's collection of the French artist's ceramic works.*

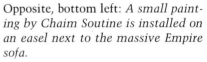

27
VISUAL POWER

"Life enhanced by art." Rene Sasselin

High over the East River, Asher Edelman's vast, high-ceilinged apartment is primarily a showcase for the collection he has put together over the last three decades. Edelman, whose activities as a Wall Street investor and arbitrageur have brought him a wide range of publicity in the last few years, also has gained a reputation as an avid collector of contemporary art. But his interest in art began long before his financial activities had made him a familiar name on the business-news pages. He remembers collecting art books when he was twelve or thirteen years old, and he started looking at objects in museums when he was a teenager. As an undergraduate at Bard College, he bought prints and drawings from other students. "The first painting I bought, when I was twenty-one, was by one of my Bard classmates," he says. "And I remember that when I was working as a bartender in college, I saw a Jackson Pollock painting that I really coveted. But it was $8,000 and that seemed like an unobtainable fortune then."

Things are different these days. Edelman, who according to several dealers was the first to pay over a million dollars for a work by Frank Stella, can afford to collect at high levels. The work he favors is at once vigorous and contemplative. The front hallway of his recently refurbished apartment holds one of Robert Morris's apocalyptic new paintings—an abstract firestorm of color framed by plaster casts of body parts that marries images of reproduction and destruction—and two minimalist compositions by Donald Judd. In the gallery-like main hallway hangs a striking portrait of the collector with attendant layered images by David Salle, also paintings by Richard Artschwager and Nabil Nahas, and a huge recent Stella construction. At the end of the fifty-seven-foot space stands a monumental Roman bronze male figure, a true *pièce de resistance*. Its brooding energy is in surprising harmony with the surrounding twentieth century art. Connecting hallways are sites for drawings by Brice Marden, Cy Twombly, Salle, and Sandro Chia.

Monochromatic pictures are grouped in the large living room, which is sparcely furnished with two sofas and a few small tables. The larger sofa, with its dramatic shape and high back, once belonged to Christian Dior. For Dior it was flashily covered in brown satin; now it is upholstered in a more restrained grey

wool. On the north wall of the room an enormous dark grey-and-white painting by Cy Twombly entirely fills the space. Like many of the overscale works in the apartment, it had to be hoisted in from the street since the apartment building elevator was too small to accomodate it. A vintage black painting and a large, silvery construction, both by Frank Stella, a subtle white scribble by Twombly, and Jasper Johns' fugue-like, autobiographical meditation, "Winter," also hang in this room. The overall effect is of harnessed visual power, of art as the attainment of stark harmony and control over matter.

In the dining room there is more color—art exuding energy. Constructions by John Chamberlain, Frank Stella, and Haim Steinbach protrude from the walls, with a boxed sculpture by Thomas Lanigan-Schmidt nearby. The dining room table—a sheet of rectangular glass supported by a multicolored wooden base constructed of curved, jig-saw-puzzle-like elements—was designed and made by sculptor George Sugarman. Bentwood chairs painted in shades of red, yellow, purple, and green go with the table. The flecks of random color in the custom-designed area rug under the table reflect a palette that harmonizes with the table and chairs. A small breakfast room adjoins the dining room. It contains an elegantly plain American art deco table, sideboard, and chairs, and some of the twentieth century silver that Edelman has continued to collect, also a suite of lyrical Twombly drawings. "It's one of my favorite places in the apartment," says Edelman. "I like its serenity and intimacy."

A corner library, with honey-colored panelling and windows on two sides, is also an intimate room. Works by Rauschenberg, Miro, and Chia hang there. The leather sofas—reproductions of designs by Jean Michel Frank—French art deco side tables, and a suite of two chairs and a small, round table by Josef Hoffmann reflect Edelman's growing interest in the decorative arts. He says that his wife, Regina, has stimulated him to look more closely at furniture and objects, beyond his longtime interest in the Venini glass of the 1950s and finely designed French twentieth century silver.

With little formal education in art history—"I took a course in Renaissance painting and studied a little nineteenth century French painting at Bard"—Edelman has taught himself by constant observation. "I'm much more interested in looking at paintings than in reading," he says. "I began buying art because I wanted to take it home, hang it up, and look at it over time. During the 1960s and early 1970s, it was hard to find avant-garde art in museum collections. I would often buy things by artists who weren't that well established. I believed in what they were doing and I wanted to support their efforts. Sometimes I also bought things from dealers whose goals interested

Above: *A sofa that once belonged to Christian Dior is one of the few pieces in the collector's living room. The 1958 Jasper Johns "Grey Painting with Ball" is a work the collector once sold only to buy it back within the year. Behind the sofa, a small sculpture by American artist David Smith.*

Right: *The breakfast room contains a serene art deco sideboard and a suite of drawings by Cy Twombly. On the sideboard, a silver coffee service designed by architect Hans Holhein in 1984 reflects the collector's longtime interest in silver of the twentieth century.*

David Salle's powerful and unusual portrait of Asher Edelman dominates the collector's gallery-like apartment hallway. Also installed in this space are a recent monumental relief by Frank Stella and a Roman bronze male figure.

me. I wanted to support what they were doing as well." Collecting really became what Edelman calls "a killer drive." "My goal hasn't been investment," he says. "I've sold very little." At one point, however, he did sell some of his major, earlier pieces. "I wanted to try to start fresh, to begin again with the art of the 1980s. But after I sold one Johns, I bought it back within the year. I just missed it too much! I also had sold a Picasso painting that I missed. Instead, I found myself buying a Picasso drawing of Dora Maar. It's even more complete and beautiful than the Picasso painting." Edelman, whose collection now totals more than 400 works, says he does weed out the collection each year. "If I've bought a lot of pictures by one artist, I sometimes sell some of them after I consider how the work is progressing. I like to look at something for at least a year. We rotate things quite often, changing what is hung and where things are installed. There are about fifty things in the apartment at any given time. And I hardly ever sell more than ten things a year."

Edelman employs an administrator to keep track of the objects in the collection. He also worked with lighting engineer Rick Shaver on the complex lighting system for the apartment. It consists of fixed, point lighting that is nevertheless highly flexible. Each fixture can be redirected or actually changed to accomodate more than twenty different kinds of light bulbs and plug-in fixtures. He protects his collection by using ultraviolet resistant shades and has had the windows specially coated with an ultra-violet light-resistant substance. Edelman is cautious about loaning works to museum exhibitions, having had some damaged in the course of travel.

Rarely seeking the advice of others about what he buys, Edelman has become a collector confident in his own taste, his own eye. He has bought aggressively and cleverly, and has found auctions a good source for currently unfashionable works. "I have bought all my Walter De Maria sculptures from recent auctions," he says. "But it's getting tougher. The contemporary market seems more and more inflated by a lot of ignorance,

Opposite: *Four contemporary sculptured heads dominate a library table. Over the mantel, Miro's great 1927 "Portrait."*

Left: *The library is furnished with designs by Jean Michel Frank, Alberto Giacometti, and Josef Hoffmann, along with small art deco pieces.*

and you really see it at these auctions where people will pay too much for almost anything." He still spends considerable time looking at work in New York galleries but relies increasingly on an international network of significant dealers who offer contemporary work. "I now find things in France, Switzerland, Italy. Dealers like Bruno Bischofsberger in Switzerland and Lucio Amelio have shown me wonderful art. And I like to look in Paris. There still is not much interest in contemporary art in Paris and sometimes work is more available there."

Lately, too, both Edelman and his wife have become fascinated with antiquities. They now own ancient Celtic, Roman, Greek, and Egyptian objects, and they plan to spend part of their summer in Crete on an archeological dig. "I've been buying antiquities for the last five years," says Edelman. "It's a learning process. We've been reading catalogues, meeting dealers, and mostly studying the objects themselves. Contemporary art hasn't stopped interesting me, but these days I think that collecting antiquities may be even more interesting."

Another Stella relief is installed in the dining room, which is furnished with multicolored chairs and a table designed by George Sugarman.

28
CONTEMPORARY ART IN HAWAII, FOLK ART IN VERMONT

"Buying the work of contemporary artists before they become famous . . . is undoubtedly the most hazardous of all forms of collecting. It offers the maximum of excitement, partly because it must always be something of a gamble, partly because the art of our time affects us more strongly than the art of the past." Sir Kenneth Clark

Thurston and Laila Twigg-Smith seem to have an appetite for art and objects that grows even as it is fed. They have quickly filled two homes at opposite ends of the United States with the results of their enthusiastic collecting. Each of these col-lections reflects very different concerns, but both display an irrepressible exuberance, curiosity, and a willingness to seek out untried art.

The couple's permanent home is an airy modern house near Diamond Head that embraces a spectacular view of Honolulu complete with swaying palms and a distant, sail-flecked ocean. They also maintain an old farmhouse in eastern Vermont that was once the country retreat of writer Sinclair Lewis. Thurston Twigg-Smith, who is owner and publisher of Honolulu's news-paper, *The Advertiser*, is from one of Hawaii's first missionary families. His great-aunt, in fact, was the first white child born on the Hawaiian Islands. His father was an artist whose paint-ings are coveted objects in Hawaii. Laila, a working artist who came to the islands from California in the late 1960s, received her art degree from San Jose State University and is also a mu-seum administrator and curator. She met her husband when she applied for a job as curator of the art gallery maintained and operated by the newspaper.

Their Honolulu house, all white walls and terraces opening out directly from rooms on two different levels, is packed with colorful and unusual paintings and sculptures by an unusually diversified range of contemporary artists. Much of the art the

Through the patio and gallery of the Twigg-Smiths' Hawaiian house one sees three David Hockney drawings ("Mexican Hotel" series) and one of Neil Jenney's "Atmo-sphere" paintings hanging near the grand piano.

couple has collected is by contemporary West Coast artists—paintings and works on paper by William Wiley, Ed Ruscha, David Hockney, and Charles Garabedian; sculpture by Robert Hudson, Roy De Forrest, Robert Woodrow, John Buck (who now lives part of the year in Hawaii), Viola Frey, Stephen de Staebler, Manuel Neri, and Tony Berlant. Several large figures of horses, constructed from twigs or fragments of metal by Deborah Butterfield, graze on the patios, and there are paintings by such diverse artists as Pat Steir, Tom Wesselmann, Alex Katz, Cy Twombly, Milton Avery, Neil Jenney, Lowell Nesbitt, Robert Kushner, John Alexander, Izhar Patkin, and Georgia O'Keeffe.

Art is also incorporated into the house in many different ways. There is a Robert Rauschenberg enamel panel installed near the front door, and a bronze relief robe by Jim Dine. Witty marine-life-derived metal reliefs by Mark Bulwinkle ("he paints with a blow torch") were commissioned by the Twigg-Smiths as decorative elements around the roofs of their porches, and a bronze sunbather by Duane Hanson lounges beside the swimming pool. The figure is so startlingly lifelike that guests have been known to call out to her from the terrace above.

"This is an intuitive collection," says Laila Twigg-Smith, who cheerfully admits that "we've been buying wildly ever since the early 1980s. We are collectors by nature. What happens is that you run into things you love, and you can't resist them."

The entire house testifies to those collecting instincts, which have ranged from Scandinavian Christmas plates to tramp art, but the main focus of the collection is ebullient, colorful, recent American painting and sculpture. The Twigg-Smiths now have several hundred works, and their house seems to be expanding constantly to provide new space for the collection. They also maintain a separate collection for the newspaper offices, and works from both collections were designated for the new museum of contemporary art scheduled to open in Honolulu in the fall of 1988.

The couple has been instrumental in the founding and building of this museum—The Contemporary Museum at Spalding House—whose construction was well underway at the time of our visit. The grand old house was once Thurston Twigg-Smith's home. When it is finished, it will contain a collection that surveys the art of the past forty years on what Thurston describes as "a rolling basis." He and his wife have worked relentlessly to make this museum a reality; indeed they were the first to suggest such an institution to the island. The permanent collection will include at least a thousand works, many of them contributed by the Twigg-Smiths.

Laila says that one of the things she has most enjoyed has been sharing their collection with the people of Hawaii. "There just isn't much contemporary art here to see," she points out.

The Twigg-Smiths' Vermont farmhouse, a complete contrast to their Hawaiian home, is filled with sub-collections of objects installed according to similarities of category and form. Advertising signs, painted game boards, trivets, and tools are formally grouped on walls throughout this eighteenth century house which once belonged to Sinclair Lewis.

But having such a collection in Hawaii poses certain unusual challenges. The collectors are not in a position to spend weekends wandering through art galleries. Instead, they must travel constantly, making frequent trips to San Francisco and Los Angeles, as well as to New York and Europe. They point out that visits to the large art fairs are extremely useful as a way to see a great deal of contemporary art in a limited amount of time. They also keep in touch through voracious reading of art-related publications and exhibition catalogues. "Twigg annotates everything for me to check on," says Laila. "He is an incredible researcher." They have found that buying from slides or reproductions is an unsatisfactory method and now avoid it. They have also discovered that shipping their works of art across the Pacific amounts to a costly bit of collecting overhead. "It's very expensive," says Laila, "and we end up with dozens of these expensive crates that we then have to figure out how to store or reuse. Lately, we've put some outside the newspaper warehouse, hoping that people will come along and take them."

Another problem the collectors contend with is the unusually destructive climate of Hawaii. Tropical humidity, salt-laden air, and other conditions that speed up organic decay are a given of the location. "We have to be realistic about where we live," says Laila. "We often don't buy drawings because of the climate, and we have had our share of conservation problems. But we love the art and we want to live with it, so we try to take what precautions we can towards its preservation." There is a curator who helps look after the private collection and another who handles the corporate collection. The couple has also built a museum-quality storage room in the house itself.

The Twigg-Smith Vermont vacation house holds an entirely different kind of collection. What is installed there is based on a love of the region and an interest in folk art and the anonymous products of the area. "It was appropriate to collect Americana," says the couple. They searched through antique barns, went to every auction they heard of or read about, and drove hundreds of miles through the state and around neighboring states to find things. The house is filled with the results of their excursions. Groups of painted metal doorstops in the shape of bouquets; arrangements of trivets, tools, carved fish, ceramics, heart-shaped objects, and folk-art boxes—all enliven virtually every surface of the house. Also prominent are the modern folk-art painted saws of Jacob Cass. It is an irrepressibly personal collection, bursting with energy and demonstrating the couple's lively fascination with man-made artifacts of a humble nature. The Twigg-Smiths bring great imagination and individuality to their collecting activities and have never been fettered by an attachment to any prevailing taste other than their own.

Two views of the spacious Hawaiian living room shows the Twigg-Smiths' love for exhuberant contemporary art. Works by Alex Katz, Janis Provisor, Cy Twombly, and Manuel Neri are among the paintings and sculptures that line the living room and hall. The large abstraction is Diebenkorn's "Ocean Park #47." A Michael Taylor-designed lamp provides a decorative sculptural accent.

Opposite top: Another view of the living room where the collectors have installed paintings by William Wiley and Jennifer Bartlett. The standing figure is by Jonathan Borofsky. The wood wall piece is H. C. Westermann's "Exclamation Mark." On the left wall, a portrait relief by John Ahearn.

Opposite bottom: Ed Ruscha's "Wildcats of the World," a seated figure ("Maria") by sculptor John de Andrea, and Westermann's enlarged tic-tac-toe sculpture with its intentionally misplaced "X" are installed in the master bath.

Above: *In the den, more of John Buck's wood figures are grouped on a shelf over an illuminated painting by Izhar Patkin. To the right, David Bates's painting, "Fisherman," looms before a lifelike sculpture of a bulldog.*

Opposite: *A metal box collage by California sculptor Tony Berlant and John Buck's koa-wood standing figure are placed in front of a 90-foot long painting by Charles Garabedian in the gallery space constructed off an outdoor patio and porch.*

29

AN ATTRACTION TO
THE PAINTERLY

*"That balanced combination of the useful and the
beautiful, of prosperity and good breeding . . ."*
John Summerson

The apartment of this prominent New York businessman and his wife, an art historian and former educator, eloquently displays a disciplined passion for modern and contemporary art. Although their collection of American modernist pictures and European and American contemporary art was started fifteen years ago with the purchase of a Charles Burchfield landscape, its development has been both swift and decisive. It is a focused collection, directed by a penchant for works with a strong painterly quality. Sculpture in the collection also demonstrates this predeliction for surface textures, a complex interplay of volume and void, and poetic or dramatic content.

By 1986 the collection had become such a primary part of the couple's life that it impelled them to reconsider the spatial arrangement of their apartment. "The children had grown up and moved out, the number of art works had grown to nearly a hundred, and it was time for a change. The paintings needed a cooler environment. They also needed more walls and better vantage points with more space."

So they moved to other quarters for over a year while the apartment was virtually gutted, patterned wallpapers were removed, spaces were drastically enlarged and simplified, and new lighting was installed. Close collaboration between the collectors and their architect Robert Leibreich produced a gracious and livable series of interiors that are also unusually hospitable to a varied art collection which includes demanding and large-scale works. A cleanly designed, impressively spacious entrance gallery suitable for major works is the setting for sculptures by Bryan Hunt and Joel Shapiro, with paintings by Jennifer Bartlett, Robert Moskowitz, Donald Sultan, Graham Nickson, and Gregory Amenoff. All the contemporary pictures share energetic brushwork and extremely strong painterly ideas.

This enlarged foyer leads to a more traditionally decorated living room whose moldings were left intact. It contains a newly installed nineteenth century marble mantelpiece. Muted wall color is the backdrop to paintings by Georgia O'Keeffe, Milton Avery, Marsden Hartley, Charles Demuth, Edward Hopper, Niles Spencer, Arthur Dove, and Oscar Bluemner—all significant American modernists. Decorators Tom Fleming and Keith Irvine chose the twin nineteenth century ebony Regency sofas to compliment the glowing paintings on the walls. Though the family's taste is for modern art, they have chosen comfortably traditional and unobtrusive furniture as a foil for their artworks.

The collectors decided to install track lighting in order to preserve the ceiling heights necessary for accomodating large contemporary paintings, since recessed fixtures would have meant lowered ceilings. In collaboration with the architect, they also planned a restructuring of part of the apartment's bedroom wing to allow for a large, octagonal gallery suitable for major works by Ellsworth Kelly and Roy Lichtenstein, with enough room for free-standing sculpture by Jackie Ferrara. A structural column that remained off center in this new gallery created a challenging spatial issue that was resolved by commissioning sculptor Ned Smyth to design a mosaic casing especially for that column. "Smyth amazed the installation crew when he came in to install the mosaic." the collectors recall. "The work went smoothly and quickly; the pieces fit together perfectly. That showed them a thing or two about precision craftsmanship and the integrity of the artist."

Commissioning the piece was a new experience for the couple. "We thought the drawings looked fine, but how do you know what something will look like when it's realized? We would not have had the knowledge or the courage to commission something when we started collecting. Experience in looking, judging, and buying allowed us to know that Smyth was the right artist for that particular project."

Their most recently undertaken commission was a new dining room table designed by Scott Burton. Known for his monumentally scaled art works for public spaces, this innovative sculptor rarely accepts domestic commissions, but he was enthusiastic about this project. "Since Scott had become very interested in working with wood, he liked the idea of making a table for us," say the collectors, both long-time admirers of Burton's work. The piece—actually a matched pair of mahogany tables with structurally arresting legs—elegantly marries abstract sculptural ideas with traditional materials. The tables are also functionally flexible. Their sculptural strengths are complemented by the other works of art in the room. A serene, highly personal painting by Nicholas Africano, an abstract canvas by the British painter John Walker, a small, poetic head from sculptor Christopher Wilmarth's Mallarmé series, John Alexander's searingly ironic work, and a metal wall piece by Donald Judd hang on the parchment-papered walls of the dining room.

A gallery designed for large contemporary works was a major change in this New York apartment when the collectors remodelled the space. This view shows a black-and-white painting by Ellsworth Kelly, a sculpture by Jackie Ferrara, and a column whose mosaic covering is by Ned Smyth.

Two views of the living room where the collectors have installed works by major twentieth century American artists. Paintings by Georgia O'Keeffe, Milton Avery, Marsden Hartley, and Edward Hopper are complemented by elegant European furniture. Hopper's painting of a Cape Cod farmhouse hangs beside an American Impressionist landscape by John H. Twachtman. In front of these works is a sculpture by Joel Shapiro.

162

Above: *Jennifer Bartlett's four-part, diamond-shaped canvas, "Pisces: Dark Star," is installed in a corner of the library. Deep red walls set off contemporary paintings in this room.*

Left: *The apartment entrance hall is another display area for over-size contemporary art. It is dominated by Bryan Hunt's bronze sculpture, "Dancing."*

Following page: *Twin dining room mahogany tables were designed by sculptor Scott Burton to be used separately or together. A Donald Judd metal wall sculpture and a painting by John Walker contrast with the dark wood of the table.*

Such a temperamentally variegated combination of work expresses a remarkable range in contemporary art. It also demonstrates a commitment to very distinct artistic ideas. The couple is united and unusually thoughtful in their approach to making acquisitions. "We must both agree before we buy anything," is a cardinal rule. "We have never been influenced to buy because of trends. We look carefully and at length before we make our decisions."

Certain unexpected and sometimes disconcerting experiences have taught these collectors the hidden expenses in collecting. In one instance the cost of conservation work on a painting damaged while out on exhibition equalled the original price of the picture. Another unforeseen expense, they found, could be the cost of moving sculptures and large pictures within an apartment. More than once they have sought the help of professional art movers to reposition sculpture or rehang paintings. Storage space outside the apartment has been another additional cost. "There is only room for about seventy-five works in the apartment. We often change things around and keep what isn't hanging in a storage room." The new walls are covered with neutral-colored paint, fabrics, or papers. (Fabric-covered walls can make shifting and rehanging art much easier, since the fabric does not show nail holes. It also cuts down on the expense of repainting walls.)

While the collection continues to expand with additional works by contemporary artists, it also now includes recently acquired, major paintings by Severin Roesen and John H. Twachtman, as well as several small still-lifes by other nineteenth century American painters. These additions are the result of an expanding knowledge of American art history, yet another reflection of the serious commitment these collectors have to their larger vision of art.

30
A JOURNEY OF DISCOVERY

"A work of art cannot be disassociated from its historical epoch, so that it comes to represent and even to interpret the style of one period." Maurice Rheims

Chicago is a city with a history of great art collectors. Since the turn of the century, the city that nurtured Louis Sullivan and Frank Lloyd Wright has produced a tradition of independently minded, cultivated collectors who have acquired advanced European and American art with remarkable vigor and acumen.

The Buchbinder family collection, formed over the last twenty-five years, is part of this ongoing Chicago collecting tradition. The art that fills the lakeside apartment of Gilda and Henry Buchbinder is notable for its intense, sometimes shocking imagery and colors, evidence of that unique vitality associated with what has come to be called The Chicago School. The work gathered here makes palpable a particular moment of artistic ferment, originality, and productivity that erupted among Chicago painters and sculptors over two decades ago—a shared sensibility often influenced by folk art, *art brut*, surrealism, psychological issues, and an abiding interest in certain kinds of realism.

The Buchbinders had always been interested in modern architecture and design, but they only began to learn about contemporary art during the mid 1960s, after Joshua Taylor, the former director of the Smithsonian, urged them to join a group at the Chicago Art Institute that devoted itself to contemporary art. "Through that group we met a whole new range of people. We were exposed to the new galleries springing up, and we came into contact with other collectors, curators, and critics like Dennis Adrian who became close and longtime friends."

Just at this time a new generation of young Chicago painters was emerging and creating a distinct, often aggressive new artistic vocabulary. "We were drawn to the real content in these pictures," says Gilda Buchbinder. "They were difficult, but they possessed unforgettable power. Many of these images explored the dark sides of life, and their emotional quality forced you to confront things that on your own you might never have dealt with." The Buchbinders began to attend the shows mounted at the pivotal Hyde Park Art Center. "Many Chicago artists

In this view of the dining room, a sculpture by H. C. Westermann stands in the foreground; beyond it, a monumental ceramic figure, "Power Blue Suit," by Viola Frey, and a painting of two nudes by Philip Pearlstein.

Overall views of the living room demonstrate the power and diversity of this Chicago collection. Roger Brown, William Wiley, and Ed Paschke are artists represented in depth. In the second view, paintings by Brown, Philip Hanson, and Robert Barnes dominate, along with sculptures by Westermann; included among the latter, on the table by the sofa, is his "Come Off It, Jackie." On the coffee table is Roger Brown's "Ambulance Iron." Seen on the far wall of the dining room is a 1976 portrait of Mrs. Buchbinder by Philip Pearlstein.

attended these exhibitions, and it was there that many of them got their first opportunity to publicly present their work." In the midst of the political, social, regional, and psychological ferment of the 1960s, the Buchbinders found themselves meeting artists and seeing their work in their studios before they had galleries to represent them. Ed Paschke was one such artist. The Buchbinders also saw the provocative, silhouetted narratives of Roger Brown, and became familiar with the quirky constructions of H. C. Westermann, an older artist whose importance also began to emerge at this time. At the Frumkin Gallery they became familiar with Westermann, with New York painter Philip Pearlstein, and with other challenging new work by painters like Jack Beal. They added paintings by Philip Hanson, Barbara Rossi, Jim Nutt, and Christina Ramburg to their collection. Collectors and artists became close friends who would exchange artistic discoveries in an ongoing social life. "People would share the excitement. Artists told us about the drawings of folk artist Joseph Yoakum and the Snap Wyatt side show banners. Together we discovered the fanciful birdhouse constructions of Aldo Piacenza, a Chicago outsider artist."

Hank Buchbinder recalls that when he saw the profuse way Dennis Adrian hung his pictures, "It challenged all my ideas of Bauhaus good taste and made it possible for me to accept some of the tougher art we were seeing." The couple, who made it a policy to agree on whatever they acquired, looked at art for its visual interest and learned to avoid precious things. "If a work reveals itself too quickly, it becomes decorative. We've always picked the toughest and largest works." The collection contains a substantial number of major works by Brown, Westermann, Pearlstein, Paschke, and Karl Wirsum, including painted portraits of every member of the family by Paschke. The strong patterns, colors, and content of the works in this collection are complemented by vibrant Kilim rugs and pieces of classic modern furniture.

Art and artifacts co-exist in this home with a richness that goes beyond any conventional idea of good taste. "Our involvement with a vital slice of American art history really just happened," says Gilda Buchbinder. "Living in the middle of a particular art movement, as we have done, we are now often shocked at the discrepancies between what we experienced, what we remember happening, and what critics and historians now write about that time. Often we are aware of the personal meanings embedded in the work, something you can only know if you were there when they were being made."

Opposite: *The breakfast alcove contains several panoramic photographs by Eugene Omar Goldbeck, a Texan who made his living photographing large groups of people. A Hollywood print by Ed Ruscha and an arrangement of lead models for spoons are also displayed.*

Above: *In the apartment dining room, an allegorical portrait of Mrs. Buchbinder by Richard Willenbrink, a Chicago painter known for his highly symbolic style, hangs near "Man with Unnecessary Burden," a ceramic self-portrait by Robert Arneson, and an early painting of a wrestler by Ed Paschke. Beneath the Paschke, another Westermann construction.*

Opposite: *The library is furnished with classic modern furniture by Corbusier and Mies van der Rohe. Folk art figures and works by Karl Wirsum, Jack Beal, and Claes Oldenburg are installed with a drawing by Rafael Ferrer and a 1982 portrait of Gilda Buchbinder by Ed Paschke. Over the mantel, Karl Wirsum's "Eye Browse."*

Above: *The dining room table holds Westermann's "Exotic Garden." Folk art children's chairs and birdhouses built by Aldo Piacenza are arranged beneath a shelf containing Amazon Indian artifacts and ancient Amazon and Peruvian tomb pieces. Roger Brown's "Welcome Home: An Approach from the Far Northwest" hangs over the shelf.*

Left: *A graphite portrait of Mrs. Buchbinder by Kent Twitchell and Roger Brown's "Lady and the Duck," the artist's first picture to incorporate a full-sized figure, hang in the master bedroom with Pearlstein's "Nudes with Bentwood Bench" and a print of an Arneson self-portrait.*

31
EXTRAVAGANTLY PERSONAL

*"The surroundings become a museum of the soul,
an archive of its experiences." Mario Praz*

It is difficult if not self-defeating to try and separate Sherry and Alan Koppel's art collection from its surroundings. Assembled with knowledge, flair, and an obvious *joie de vivre,* the highly personal, integrated environment these young Chicago collectors have created combines contemporary art and twentieth-century decorative arts with a dramatic sense of interior design.

The Koppels' involvement with art began early. The couple met when both were art students at Ohio State University. Married while still in college, "we were already altering our surroundings," Sherry says. "In some way, our marriage was a collaboration of taste."

Alan Koppel is now a commodities trader at Chicago's Mercantile Exchange. Sherry turned from painting to become a colorist who advised clients on possible color schemes for interior decoration. She set up her own costume jewelry company five years ago. Her unusual flair for color, shape, and composition—evident in how the couple's art collection is both chosen and displayed—has made her company, Diva, a success from the beginning. "When my partner and I started Diva, we went to Providence, Rhode Island, the Paris of beads, and just bought thousands of beads. The supplier thought we were nuts—what would we do with them all?—so we came back to Chicago and made these hundreds of necklaces. And people loved them."

The pre-war Chicago apartment where Sherry and Alan live with their two sons, their dog Sadie, and their formidable parrot, Man Ray (named after William Wegman's late canine model), has been transformed over the years into an arrestingly theatrical setting for their continually evolving collection. The front hall and dining room are painted in glamorous dark colors, and another, copper-colored hallway leads to the couple's black-walled bedroom. A sumptuous, wood-panelled den contrasts with the elegant living room, which has slate-blue carpets and ivory-painted walls that modulate hues as the light shifts.

The Koppels are the rare example of collectors who embrace rather than shun adventurous background colors, textures, and unique furniture pieces for their art. Their unusually sophisticated flair for creating dramatic decor reflects an innate un-derstanding of artistic process and emphasizes a liberated imagination. Says Sherry, "Everything looks richer on a colored wall. I've also had an ongoing strong attraction to dark colors. I think of white as a primer."

A striking Bugatti shelf is a sculptural element in the dark-blue foyer. The front hall contains a primitivistic Karl Wirsum puppet, a painting by Ed Paschke, and a gem-like Nam June Paik television piece—a miniature of his "Exotic Garden," where small television sets glow in the midst of tropical foliage. A large, poetic, "altered chair" sculpture by Chicago artist Margaret Wharton shares the space with a bronze sculpture by Jonathan Silverman and a small, Dutch-designed, early twentieth century table-and-chair set, also a psychologically charged Eric Fischl painting which the Koppels bought in the mid-seventies, before the artist was well known.

The most magical object in the dining room may be "The Dodo Bird Museum," an intricately constructed piece that is half Gothic doll house and half belltower. Liberally covered with irridescent feathers, it is the creation of the young New York artist David Beck. The room also includes a horse sculpture of twigs by Deborah Butterfield, an extraordinary suite of French garden chairs from the 1930s, and a table Sherry designed. On a Bugatti table in the corner stands Sherry's small collection of nineteenth century neo-classical candlesticks, complementing another group of silver tea sets. Some of these sets are contemporary designs by Michael Venturi, Ettore Sottsass, and Morris Graves, others are from the 1930s.

The library is rich with a variety of visual incidents, from sculptures, photographs, and paintings to Alan's robot collection and various fine art deco lamps and tables, also an imposing Bugatti throne chair and a zebra-striped rug that cleverly echoes the pattern in a Wegman photograph of his dog Man Ray painted up as a zebra. A selection of fabulously colorful featherwork turns out not to be American Indian. Alan says the pieces are from Amazonian Indian tribes who still create the intricate ornaments and headdresses. "I realized that this work was as beautiful as many American Indian things and that it was still plentiful and reasonable in price when I bought it. It was coming from a living culture." They have also acquired several choice examples of American Plains Indian art over the years.

The Koppels have successfully combined furniture of exceptional design with their collection of art and objects. A main source for their Bugatti furniture and their pieces from the twenties and thirties has been Bud Holland, a dealer in twentieth century decorative arts and one of the Chicago collecting community's special assets.

"I don't buy for investment; I gamble every day in the commodities market," says Alan. "I think there's nothing wrong

The deep grey-browns of the Koppels' dining room are backdrop for the collectors' recently restored suit of Samurai armor, their David Beck construction, "The Dodo Bird Museum," and a horse by sculptor Deborah Butterfield. The dining room table was designed by Mrs. Koppel and John Corcoral, and the chairs are French garden chairs.

Above: *In the apartment hallway the collectors have hung an early painting by Eric Fischl, an Ed Paschke painting, and Andy Warhol's triple Marilyn portrait. A chair sculpture by Chicago sculptor Margaret Wharton playfully echoes the forms of the early twentieth century Dutch-desgined modernist chairs and the table with its sculpture by Donald Lipski.*

Right: *The deep black walls of the master bedroom are a foil for Ed Paschke's thirtieth birthday portrait of Sherry Koppel and an elaborate Indian feather work. The inlaid desk is by Bugatti.*

Opposite top: *The panelled library combines an art deco coffee table, lamps, and ceiling fixture with the eccentric forms of a great Bugatti chair and a chair made from animal horns. Mr. Koppel's collection of robots is arranged on the bookshelves to the left of William Wegman's photographs of a zebra-striped Man Ray.*

Opposite bottom: *The formal living room combines elegantly grouped Egyptian revival furniture, art deco, and placques that illustrate scenes from Edgar Allen Poe's stories. A black-and-white painting by Jim Nutt, called "Seems Simple," is a complex visual riddle.*

174

with getting something you eventually tire of, but I now try to consider specific works in the light of the artist's long-term achievements. We recently sold much of the photography collection we had put together over the years. The vintage prints had become extremely valuable, so much so that we felt we shouldn't hold on to them. Collecting is our kind of cultural entertainment, and I believe it should be a pleasurable thing. Many collectors are so serious, they seem to feel they are more important than the artist or the art."

Sherry believes that placement of things "is also a part of the creative process. Unless you move things around, it's like living in a museum, and we definitely don't live in a museum. We need to feel the spirit through the art. It's a fundamental thing

to us." She says that her sons have developed strong visual opinions from living with such challenging art.

Although they maintain ties to local artists like Paschke and Wharton, the Koppels have not limited themselves to Chicago artists. And while they buy in New York and Chicago, they like being at a remove from New York, feeling that it helps edit their thinking. They also like to buy before an artist has become popular. "It's economic reality," says Alan. "Too much contemporary art has become too expensive." Lately the Koppels have found themselves increasingly involved in the decorative arts—a field "where you can still make exciting discoveries"—consistent with their guiding philosophy of collecting as a personal passion: "We collect to please ourselves."

One of Nam June Paik's major television installations enlivens the hallway between the apartment bedrooms. The series of sets is left running and its images are hypnotic.

32
A COLLECTOR OF THE MOMENT

"When I'm looking at the works Gerry has collected, I feel I'm looking at the artist at his or her very best." I. Michael Danoff.

Chicago collector Gerald S. Elliott lives with his choice examples of modern and contemporary art high above the city in a white-walled apartment whose every surface is a repository for art. His glowing examples of minimalist, new image and neo-expressionist paintings and sculpture almost make visitors ignore the splendid view of Lake Michigan stretching to the horizon some seventy floors below. A lawyer now in his early fifties, Elliott says that his interest in "art and collecting has become obsessive, all pervasive. I love it. It's the most important thing in my life."

The ambitious and discerning collection now contains over a hundred works, most of them from the 1960s, 1970s and 1980s. Having managed to acquire a dozen or more prime examples of Abstract Expressionist painting through the early 1970s—including works by Mark Rothko, Clyfford Still, Barnett Newman, and Willem de Kooning—Elliott began to feel that "the prices of what I owned had become disproportionate to my own net worth." In order to get them, he had already taken out back loans and a second mortgage on his house. After deciding he wanted to commit himself to the works of younger artists, he sold a major part of the Abstract Expressionist collection and has never regretted it. Instead he looks back on the sale as "a way to freedom." The proceeds gave him the kind of stake he needed to go after the art of his own time. "I want to be part of the current fray," he explains. "I enjoy collecting the work of people who are alive, and I am happy to be in a field where I believe I can make a mark. I want a museum-quality collection."

From 1976 until the early 1980s, Elliott concentrated on acquiring minimalist works, and around 1982 he began to focus on the emerging generation of neo-expressionist artists. Recently he has been considering the consumer-smart works of yet another generation of "neo-geo" New York painters and sculptors. Though he now owns one of Jeff Koons's 1985 controversial basketball "floatation pieces" (three basketballs suspended in liquid in a fish tank), he is still assessing this new

work. He also currently owns three paintings by David Salle, six by Julian Schnabel, three by Anselm Kiefer, five by Mimmo Paladino, four by Robert Longo, and fourteen works by Francesco Clemente. He still retains major paintings by Rothko and Still along with examples of the early, middle, and recent sculptures of Bruce Nauman, Richard Serra, Donald Judd, and a similar range of works by Sol LeWitt, Robert Mangold, and Neil Jenney. He owns three sculptures by Joel Shapiro, also examples of the best efforts of Susan Rothenberg, Jonathan Borofsky, and Malcolm Morley. Recently, he acquired a pair of monumental bronze doors filled with intricately arranged and modelled satirical figures made by the young artist Tom Otterness, which he installed between his capacious living room and a smaller den. He also owns pieces by the latest generation of young British sculptors, among them Tony Cragg, Richard Deacon, Bill Woodrow, and Anish Kapoor.

Elliott has an equally strong ability to perceive painting and sculpture, an unusual sensibility for a collector. He sees his abiding interest in minimal art as an extension of his early love for Abstract Expressionism. His figurative art of the 1980s he views as "a metaphor for man's situation in the '80s . . . Even the quieter works—the Brice Mardens, the Rymans, some of the LeWitts, a few of the Judds—evoke for me a kind of spiritual sense." Although he knows many of the artists and claims Malcolm Morley and the late Philip Guston as good friends, "I don't always listen to what the artists say about their works." He prefers to interpret his sculptures and canvases independently.

Lately Elliott has become more interested in special projects like the suite of canvases he recently commissioned from artist Robert Ryman. These white expanses called "The Charter Series" are now being shown as a travelling exhibition, and will be shown at the prestigious Carnegie International, but they were designed to be installed as a "meditative room" in the apartment. Despite the apartment's size, nearly twenty percent of Elliott's collection is on long-term loan to the Milwaukee Art Museum, and another twenty-five percent is on loan to various travelling exhibitions. Elliott's ultimate ambition is to have formed a late-twentieth-century collection of such focused quality that it can be left to a museum.

He has forged his opinions through years of endless reading and looking. In the mid-1970s, he took courses in art history at the University of Chicago, hoping to get a Master's Degree, until the pressures of his law practice intervened.

"My partners practically disowned me," he says. "I was spending too much time studying art!" He still subscribes to and reads a dozen art magazines and gets scores of catalogues, and his "art network" is maintained by daily telephone conversa-

Opposite: *Collector Gerald S. El-liott has filled his apartment living room with major works of con-temporary art. A 1961 sculpture by Carl Andre contrasts the curving shapes of a group of porcelain ves-sels by British ceramist Lucy Ries. Joel Shapiro's sculpture of a figure poised on one leg, and bronze doors by Tom Otterness (one set from an edition of nine) are juxtaposed with canvases by Philip Guston and Malcolm Morley.*

Above: *Another view of the living room, with Andre's sculpture in the foreground and a painting by Robert Mangold on left wall.*

Left: *Elliott's Rothko and his Clyf-ford Still are reminders of his ear-lier collection of Abstract Expression-ist work. Between them, a wall piece by Donald Judd is one of several in the collection of the artist's works from different periods.*

tions and trips to New York at least once a month. He feels that living in Chicago gives him an opportunity to assess new work in a more leisurely way than he might were he living in Manhattan. "It does allow you time to cool off. Living in Chicago is a double-edged sword—you may miss an important piece—but distance gives you discipline." Elliott emphasises that he also is willing to travel "to any place in the world where something artistically interesting is going on," and frequently does so in his quest to learn more about the context of art history into which he feels the work he buys must finally fit.

Elliott has no qualms about trading or selling pieces that he ultimately feels don't hold up, and he has sold things when their conservation became more of a problem than he could comfortably handle. His apartment has been extensively remodelled to hold his collection. He combined two smaller apartments, ripped out walls, enlarged hallways, sacrificed a bedroom, and built walls across long expanses of windows to provide more hanging space. His comfortable furniture, much of it from the Dunbar and Directional lines of the 1950s, is upholstered in pale whites and constructed of different kinds of woods. His simple dining room table and chairs are art-deco influenced. The apartment color scheme is planned to accentuate the incredible range of color and image provided by the art and not to compete with it. Though Elliott's energies are

Above: *Two Sol LeWitt pieces and an early canvas by Brice Marden hang in the apartment hallway.*

Right: *Two works by Clemente hang in the dining room. The one to the left is called "Two Well Known Trees" and was painted in 1983.*

Above: "Portrait of John Poynt," "Rigoletto," and "Confessions of Saint Sebastian" are the three paintings by Julian Schnabel installed together near the apartment dining room. Simple African pieces and plain upholstered furniture serve as accents to the pictures.

Left: A small pastel by Francesco Clemente is hung to the right of the Otterness doorway.

primarily directed toward his art collection, he has recently become intrigued with the pure sculptural forms of the small vessels by British ceramist Lucy Ries. He now has a small collection of her pots—"But only white ones! Those are the ones I want."

Elliott passionately enjoys the intangible net of relationships, the information gathering, and the acquisition of important pieces for his collection. He believes that the study of great collections of the past can help today's collectors focus their energies. "The old collectors didn't try to collect everything," he points out. "It's better to miss something than to make mistakes. I can wait until someone's second or third show before I decide to acquire a work. I don't need to make the discoveries." He also believes that "every collector has his 'moment'," the specific time when he is in harmony with what is happening artistically. For Elliott, collecting in the present is "the moment" where he can make an important contribution to future generations of art lovers.

Robert Longo's aggressive and startling 1984 painting/construction, "Now is the Fly," could make watching television in Elliott's library a distracting experience.

33
A SENSE OF MONUMENTAL FORM

"North America will have two art capitals—one in New York and the other called Los Angeles."
Eli Broad

Douglas Cramer is known to millions of television viewers as the producer of numerous television films and such popular series as "Love Boat," "Hotel," "Dynasty," and "The Colbys." He is also one of Los Angeles's most avid collectors with an intense commitment to contemporary art that has contributed to Los Angeles's burgeoning interest in the visual arts. Cramer's collection of more than four hundred works concentrates on American art with examples of what he calls "the modern masters"—Frank Stella, Ellsworth Kelly, Jim Dine, Robert Rauschenberg, Jasper Johns, Roy Lichtenstein, Andy Warhol—"and those I would call the contemporary, would-be masters." Among these latter younger artists Kramer includes Julian Schnabel, Bryan Hunt, David Salle, Susan Rothenberg, Joel Shapiro, and Donald Sultan. His Bel-Air home is filled with both large-scale and intimately sized works by these and other artists. And six years ago he built another house suited to his passionate commitment to contemporary art and artists.

La Quinta Norte, Cramer's house in the Santa Ynez valley, is situated on a stunningly scenic ranch property that includes several hundred acres of vineyards and various exotic animals. Far enough from Los Angeles to provide complete escape for the busy producer, it is still close enough to the city to be convenient for weekend residence. This capacious and serene house, designed by the architectural firm of Peter Choate Associates, combines Mediterranean and Southwestern influences, but its interior is a state-of-the-art example of the work of the pre-eminent California interior designer, the late Michael Taylor. Working together, Cramer and Taylor decided on the details and the furnishings for the 20,000-square-foot interior, which Cramer specifically wanted as a place that would "give space and play to art."

La Quinta Norte provides an extraordinary setting for Cramer's extensive collection. The oversized scale of Michael Taylor's massive but simple furniture and his distinctive lamps, rugs, and curtains provide an unusual foil for the powerful and large-scale paintings and antiquities collection artfully placed

A sculpture by Julian Schnabel rests against the side of the pool house at Douglas C. Cramer's ranch, La Quinta Norte.

Following page: *A view of the enormous living room where Greek, Roman, and Chinese antiquities and a rough, antique refectory table are contrasted with art that includes an early Frank Stella "wall piece" and Roy Lichtenstein's "Sleeping Muse," the artist's 1964 homage to Brancusi.*

183

Above: *Jim Dine's "Column With Rock and Axe" occupies the entrance hall to the living room.*

Opposite: *Mr. Cramer's bedroom and sitting room provide a serene setting for a delicate Calder mobile, and a painting by Jim Dine. The furniture was designed by Michael Taylor, who in close collaboration with the collector planned the interior design scheme of the house.*

throughout the house; as does the dramatic use of natural materials, like the Yosemite slate used for the floors. Not the least of the natural elements that set the house and its contents apart is the brilliant light streaming in through over-sized windows and sliding glass doors to bathe the interior and its works of art with a kind of radiant aura.

An impression of extraordinarily resolved perfectionism strikes guests when they enter a latticed courtyard, which leads seamlessly to the entrance hall with its installation of Jim Dine's primitivistic 1983 sculpture "Column with Rock and Axe" and two of Dine's drawings, as well as a medieval, wrought-iron candelabrum. The living room, with its Taylor-designed built-in seating, rush benches, sofas, and granite-topped tables, serves as showplace for a fine 1964 Roy Lichtenstein landscape, and the artist's 1983 "Sleeping Muse," a witty and touching homage to Constantin Brancusi which rests on a massive mantelpiece. Frank Stella's vivid, jagged "Montenegro II," work from 1974–1975, lends color to the room, while a chinese horse and several massive Chinese jars represent Cramer's discerning eye for antiquities. In the dining room are works by Ellsworth Kelly, Lichtenstein, a Robert Motherwell, and a cubist-inspired tea set by British ceramicist Andrew Lord. The hall beyond is devoted to several paintings and drawings by Donald Sultan.

The other wing of the house includes a smaller, more intimate study where some of Cramer's other collecting interests—mercury glass, antiquities often acquired on various film locations, and a group of rampant lion sculptures—are gathered. On the wall hangs a sensitive portrait drawing of Cramer by Andy Warhol. A curving staircase leads to a lower level of the house that contains several bedroom suites, all lavishly provided with works of art; Cramer's bedroom-sitting room has a 1963 Alexander Calder mobile and a cool Donald Judd metal wall construction done in 1980. Against the stairway wall Cramer has hung a series of Ellsworth Kelly drawings of grapevine leaves, studies for Cramer's own wine label. A downstairs sitting room features a highly colorful fish painting by Jean-Michel Basquiat and a sardonic work by Edward Ruscha. Hung unobtrusively nearby are an exquisitely tiny Robert Mangold cruciform painting and a recent construction by Haim Steinbach. Another exquisite and tiny work, in marble by Brice Marden, hangs at the bottom of the main stairway. Its minute size makes it no less impressive in this house filled with major canvases and sculpture.

Outside the house, among the beautifully landscaped gardens and boulders, positioned to look as if they had always been in place, three dramatically sited Joel Shapiro sculptures (each with its own customized, protective cover to fend off effects of the weather when the house is not in use) watch over a grotto-like pool. They are called "Leaping Man," Sunning Man," and "Sitting Man." In contrast, the Julian Schnabel sculpture leaning against a poolhouse wall seems disarmingly casual.

Even with all the space provided by La Quinta Norte, Cramer's collection has required yet more space. Last May he opened a 6,000-square-foot art warehouse on the property to accomodate some sixty other works of the Cramer Foundation collection. It is to this gallery that many visitors now come, drawn by its extraordinary display of contemporary art.

Cramer says, "I've always been a consummate collector of things—antique glass, mercury glass, English furniture, Staffordshire . . . As a child it was doorknobs, theater programs." He collected posters, reproductions, and museum postcards, until he was in his mid-twenties. At that time, in the mid-1950s, he was working in New York and had begun going to Manhattan galleries regularly, reading reviews and collecting prints by Picasso, Braque, Matisse, Giacometti, and other modern artists. In the 1960s he moved to Los Angeles, sold many of his graphic works, and became immersed in the lively Southern California art scene. "I began to collect Californians," he recalls, but then that second collection was sold as the result of his divorce, and Cramer found himself perforce with a new op-

portunity to resume collecting. This third time around, his tastes both more adventurous and refined, the producer turned to such major New York contemporary dealers as Leo Castelli, Mary Boone, Paula Cooper, Irving Blum, and Arnold Glimcher to survey the art scene of the late 1970s, and the result was his first acquisition of works by artists such as Shapiro, Schnabel, and Salle. He also began to focus and further refine his artistic tastes, admitting today that at first he had a hard time with the very art he now admires most.

Cramer's collection is unified by his response to dramatic, large-scale American works, his eye for monumental form (whatever a piece's actual size), the importance of color, and strong identity in a given work. He cites his enjoyment in meeting and entertaining artists, also their dealers and other collectors. He is an active member of the board of trustees and of the Executive Committee of the new Museum of Contemporary Art in Los Angeles, and his own foundation is dedicated to furthering the role of contemporary art in America. He has said that in another life he might wish to be an artist or own a gallery. For Douglas Cramer, contemporary art offers another world away from the pressures of his high-powered work, a world that provides a lexicon of permanent, still images in contrast to the shifting images of film.

Above: *An ancient Chinese horse is set next to Lichtenstein's 1964 landscape. To the right, another construction by Frank Stella.*

Opposite top: *A view from the dining room encompasses Donald Sultan's painting of a steer. To the right, a Lichtenstein variant on Picasso is hung above a shelf of Yosemite slate which holds cubist-inspired ceramics by Andrew Lord and a bust by Jonathan Ellis.*

Opposite bottom: *Paintings by Jean-Michel Basquiat and Ed Ruscha enliven a small downstairs sitting room. The tabletop sculpture is by John Chamberlain.*

34
A SPIRITUAL VIEW

*"The collector . . . takes it upon himself to trans-
figure things. . . . The surroundings become a museum of the soul, an archive of its experiences . . .
The ultimate meaning is to mirror man. . . ."*
Mario Praz

Edwin and Ann Janss have created a house built as a harmonious container for a superbly discriminating collection of twentieth century art and antiquities from civilizations that range from those of the Far East to the pre-Columbian and American Indian. The unassuming exterior of their home in Los Angeles—built in a largely Japanese neighborhood called Sawtelle—exemplifies their free and unpretentious spirit. It also gives few clues to the spaciousness and beauty of the simple but welcoming loft-like interior which provides gallery-like spaces for larger paintings. Designed as a series of graduated cubes, the house also contains a series of intimate spaces for a variety of art and objects in the collection. The large paintings of contemporary artists like Robert Rauschenberg and David Hockney harmoniously co-exist with groups of tiny antique figurines, pre-Columbian textiles, a superb first-phase Indian chief's blanket, and Mimbres pottery casually placed against the walls of the living room and the adjoining study. Light flows into the house from a ceiling skylight and from sliding glass doors in the study that open to a tiny Japanese garden.

Ed Janss, who developed the residential area of Thousand Oaks north of Los Angeles, has always been an inveterate world traveller and a man deeply committed to international humanitarian causes. With Los Angeles artist Tony Berlant, he established the Amerind Foundation, an organization dedicated to preserving the artistic and architectural heritage of prehistoric Southwest American Indian culture. He has also aided community work in South East Asia.

Edwin Janss's love of art has been parelleled by his passionate interest in oceanography and underwater biology. His own striking color photographs of undersea life are a result of his diving voyages. They hang in the hallway of the house across from a group of haunting collages by Joseph Cornell.

This highly personal art collection, formed slowly over more than thirty-five years, is based on a profound feeling for the expressive capabilities of the human spirit and an ability to perceive the essence of each individual piece, whatever its culture of origin. What Janss has chosen also reveals an underlying appreciation of humor and eroticism in art as well as a feeling for art's magical properties. A sculptural, collaged "Portrait of Walter Hopps" by West Coast artist Ed Kienholz is a satirical send-up of curatorial motivations and concerns. Other California artists in the collection, many of whom have been friends of the Jansses, include Wallace Berman, Bruce Connor, and George Herms. Janss has also assembled an exceptional group of works by H. C. Westermann, and possesses numerous wonderful illustrated letters from the artist, who was the collector's longtime close friend. Robert Rauschenberg's 1963 painting, "Diehard," Francis Bacon's "Vincent on the Road to Tarascon," and an early, figurative Diebenkorn painting, "Coffee" (1959), are installed in the large living and dining room, which is furnished casually with furniture of Edwin Janss's own design. A coffee table is really a large piece of plywood set on four blocks, created to display a delicate, figured Peruvian textile. A simple bookcase acts both as room divider and subtle display area for a tiny collage by Kurt Schwitters, several exquisite Cornell boxes, constructions by Wallace Berman, and a group of tiny antiquities.

In the library, a Japanese screen of exceptional power and beauty by Tawaraya Sotatsu dominates the intimate space, along with an 1896 painting by James Ensor. Ann Janss found the work of the introspective Belgian *fin de siècle* painter and fell in love with it. The collection also includes a series of Ensor's etchings. Exceptional examples of paintings by Magritte, Gorky, and Franz Kline are simply hung in the upstairs rooms. This collection of some 600 art works and objects, which continues to undergo a stringent refinement process, contains nothing but pieces that have personal significance proved by initial apparent simplicity. It is only after time and careful looking that the individual spirit and quality of the objects becomes overwhelming. A sense of completeness informs the devotion necessary to create such a collection, for art here is never cosmetic; it is a profound expression and enhancement of life.

Left: *Ancient American Indian pottery rests on the floor beneath a canvas by California painter Ed Moses.*

Below: *A magnificent Japanese screen by Tawaraya Sotatsu is displayed on a pedestal which also holds primitive sculpture. A First Phase Chief's blanket is protected by a sheet of glass on the library table.*

Above: *An enormous canvas by Sam Francis dominates the far wall of this loft-like California house. Close by, a house construction by William Christianbery and a casual arrangement of furniture chosen for comfort and utility. The large coffee table is used to display an ancient pre-Columbian textile under glass. On the table, a magic stone which will only spin in one direction. The African stool was brought back by Mr. Janss from a trip with his parents to Africa that he took over fifty years ago.*

Right: *Francis Bacon's "Vincent on the Road to Tarascon" hangs on the far right-hand wall of the living area. To the left, Robert Rauschenberg's 1963 painting "Diehard." In the hall are hung several of the collector's marine photographs.*

192

Above: *A collection of smaller objects, constructions, and antiquities is arranged in the simple shelf unit that also serves as a room divider. Works by Joseph Cornell, Wallace Berman, and others reward concentrated scrutiny.*

Left: *Another view of the main space in the house. Westermann drawings are over the sofa.*

Right: *Ed Keinholtz has skewered the attitudes and habits of the curator in his "Portrait of Walter Hopps," a brilliantly satirical sculpture. It is next to a fine late painting by Philip Guston.*

Below: *The master bedroom contains major canvases by Arshile Gorky and Franz Kline.*

35
TRACKING THE IMAGINATION OF A GREAT ARTIST

"It's useless to list all the beautiful things I've seen, with an experience of art acquired little by little." Henri de Toulouse-Lautrec

On one of their frequent trips to Europe, Herbert and Ruth Schimmel went in search of an old summer house in Taussat where Henri de Toulouse-Lautrec had often spent his vacations on the Atlantic coast of France. Herbert Schimmel knew the town and the name of the house, Villa Bagatelle, and when Lautrec had been a visitor there, but no-one could tell him where it might be or whether indeed it was still standing. On an inclement morning the Schimmels headed in their rented car for the small town on the French coast in the Arcachon Basin and entered its winding streets. "Herb kept saying, 'I'll know it when I see it,'" says his wife Ruth, "but we really had no idea of where we were going." The collector instinctively made a few turns and then drew up exactly in front of the very house they had been searching for. "It was basically unchanged and still had a sign with its name affixed to the side of the house," Herb Schimmel recalls with delight. "Sometimes I think I know Lautrec so well that I unconsciously already knew the way to that house."

Schimmel's almost mystical affinity with the great French artist is the result of a nearly forty-year involvement with Lautrec's work and life. This fascination with the man who captured the theatrical and café life of *fin de siècle* Paris in his posters and lithographs of performers, dancers, actors, and patrons has been the basis and focus of a constant and dedicated scholarship; an exploration of the artist's milieu, achievements, and existence which began in 1950 with an exhibition of Lautrec's graphic work and has culminated in a collection that also is the most fully documented assembly of the artist's letters, memorabilia, and works ever to have been gathered.

In 1950 the young businessman went to an exhibition at the Knoedler Gallery on 57th Street in Manhattan that commemorated the fiftieth anniversary of Toulouse-Lautrec's death. He was interested enough to go home and write to the gallery to ask about the prices for the prints and posters he had seen.

William Collins, later the curator of prints and drawings at the Clark Art Institute, wrote back, and sent a price list. "I had never thought you could buy things like this," Schimmel remembers. Before long, he was acquiring Lautrec's graphic work whenever he could. "We went to Parke-Bernet, we went to galleries, and we started to buy books about Lautrec." Now Herbert Schimmel has built an incomparable library of over 6,000 volumes that relate to Lautrec and to the period. In it are all the books Lautrec illustrated. Only one of Lautrec's known posters is absent from the Schimmels' collection, which also includes some 250 lithographs, 60 drawings, and 350 letters and various Lautrec memorabilia like the oriental artifacts the artist once owned. Much of the documentary material was acquired from Lautrec's descendants. The Bibliotheque Nationale in Paris owns four Lautrec letters, Schimmel points out. The Museum in Albi, Lautrec's native town, has no more than two. Over the years this interest in Lautrec's correspondence has resulted in three books Schimmel has co-edited on the letters: *The Unpublished Correspondence of Henri de Toulouse-Lautrec* and *Henri de Toulouse-Lautrec Letters*, both co-edited with Lucien Goldschmidt, and *The Henri de Toulouse-Lautrec—W. H. B. Sands Correspondence*, co-edited with Phillip Dennis Cate. Forthcoming is *Collected Letters of Toulouse-Lautrec*, which Schimmel is editing himself.

"One of the luckiest things that happened to us very early in our collecting was getting to know Lucien Goldschmidt," say the Schimmels. "He has been instrumental in our learning. Meeting the right dealer at the right time is utterly crucial when you are pursuing an interest like this." Schimmel says that as his interest grew, he decided he wanted to be the best collector of Toulouse-Lautrec. "The documentation became as important as the visual work. "I would pass up an expensive color print, for example, to get what was an essential piece of documentation." The popularity of the movie *Le Moulin Rouge* notwithstanding, Toulouse-Lautrec's art has never been as avidly collected in America as has Impressionism or the works of the other post-impressionist painters. "When we were collecting only Lautrec, we really had little competition. People laughed at us in the 1950s for collecting 'those advertising things'." They point out that in the beginning the frames for the posters often cost more than the posters themselves.

Their Lautrec collection led the Schimmels to learn French and to travel with increasing frequency to France. Soon three or four of the best French print dealers became part of their expanding network of contacts, as did members of the Lautrec family. "We've met everybody still alive who was or is involved with Lautrec. Part of every trip we take to France, Belgium, and Spain is spent on tracking down information about the art-

The Schimmels' unparalleled collection of Henri de Toulouse-Lautrec posters, drawings, letters, illustrated books, and documentation is enhanced by the collectors' understanding of the decorative arts of the fin de siècle. In the apartment living room, settees and chairs designed by the great French art nouveau furniture maker Marjorelle are grouped around a table by Gallé (the designer's signature is inlaid in the tabletop)

and lit by a Gallé chandelier. A Marjorelle sideboard is used to display art nouveau ceramics by Lachenal and Muller. The glass lamp was designed by Daum. In the corner is a bronze sculpture of the dancer Loie Fuller by Raoul Larche. Lautrec's posters depict May Belfort, Jane Avril, and other Parisian entertainers of the period.

ist. We have spent days looking for postcards that were photographs of the boat Lautrec went on, the beach where he vacationed, the hotel or bar where he visited." A few years ago, surviving members of the family threw a party for the Schimmels in the family house in Albi. On their most recent trip, the collectors made a pilgrimage to the artist's tomb in Verdelais.

"Lautrec and his world have governed our travels, led us to people we never would have met and places we never would have seen," says Herbert Schimmel. The collection has also led dealers, experts, and auctioneers to rely on the dedicated scholar's peerless library for information.

Others now use the collection for research about the autheticity of prints and posters that are going up for sale. Schimmel recalls identifying reproductions that were being sold as authentic lithographs. "If you've really studied, you can visually recognize the real things," he says, noting that "if you narrow your interests sufficiently you should know more about your subject than dealers who by necessity must have a very broad knowledge."

The influence of Lautrec and the *fin de siècle* in France has also led the Schimmels to their choice collection of works by artists of the period and artists who knew or exhibited with Lautrec. Their apartment contains several swirling sculptures of the dancer Loie Fuller, who took Paris by storm in the 1890s, and a suite of pastels of Fuller by artist Charles Maurin who showed with Lautrec and taught him some innovative printmaking techniques. There is a sketch of Rodin by Lautrec and several portraits and photographs of the artist by other artists. Even the Schimmels' early Red Grooms gouache is a portrait of Gauguin, one of Lautrec's contemporaries.

The Schimmels began to add art nouveau furniture and decorative arts to their collection after Herbert had brought home an exquisite Favrile glass cigarette container designed by Louis Comfort Tiffany. He bought it from the dealer Lillian Nassau at the beginning of the 1960s, "way before almost anyone was interested in the decorative arts of the *fin de siècle.*"

"I became a collector of the art and decorative arts of the 1890s," says Schimmel. "I realized that I wanted an environment that would have been compatible with what Lautrec would have had. He acquired art nouveau furniture, which was the modern furniture of his time, and he even visited specific furniture makers to get things made for him." When the collectors were visiting the *marche aux puces* around 1960, they were able to buy art nouveau furniture for the proverbial song. From one dealer they acquired a Guimard table and a Loie Fuller bronze that were sitting outside in the rain, as well as a settee and chairs by Marjorelle, one of the best French art nouveau cabinetmakers. They remember that "it all cost more to ship home than it did to buy it." Their apartment is filled with furniture by Marjorelle, Gallé, Bénouville and Ruhlmann. Their lamps are Gallé Tiffany and Lalique, and there are superb *fin de siècle* ceramic pieces by Delaherche, Dalpayrat, and Carabin. Sinuous plaster busts in the *fin de siècle* style, acquired from flea markets and second hand stores, early art deco rugs, and even William Morris-designed wallpaper complete the period style of the apartment. The relationship of Lautrec's art and art nouveau is demonstrated to be utterly intertwined. "The furnishings are an integral part of this collection," the Schimmels stress. "It would not be the same without this furniture and these decorative arts. These things are crucial to understanding the art itself."

Whatever current purchases the collectors make must be directly related to Lautrec—a rigorous discipline governed by a single-minded idea. "The collection has made us into biographers. And it has become the keystone of our entire lives."

Above: *The master bedroom also observes the style of the period. A modern repro-duction of a William Morris-designed floral fabric is used for curtains and bedspread.*

Following pages: *Charles Maurin's six pastels of Loie Fuller hang beside one of Maurin's oil portraits in the apartment dining room. Maurin, a contemporary of Lautrec, showed with him and introduced him to several innovative printing techniques. A set of American art deco chairs surrounds a French deco table. The centerpiece is Daum Nancy. The art nouveau clock in the apartment entrance hallway is from the French School of Nancy. The Marjorelle stand below it holds ceramics by Dalpayrat.*

AFTERWORD
by Holly Solomon

1. A Dealer's Education

I was born in Bridgeport, Connecticut, where I was raised on Norman Street and went to Bassick High School. There I had dreams of becoming a great actress and of one day owning "real oil paintings." I never imagined that my life would become intertwined with the visual arts of our time.

My first love was the stage, and when I entered Vassar College I decided to major in theater. It was at Vassar that I was first introduced to memorable twentieth century art by Alice Barber, one of Vassar's formidable faculty, who lived in her dormitory rooms surrounded by the sculpture of Alexander Calder and Jean Arp. But I became dissatisfied with the theater department, and with the college's conservative attitude during those McCarthy years, and in my junior year I transferred to Sarah Lawrence College. Yet I never forgot the exposure to art Miss Barber gave me. She was my first example of how it was possible for an ordinary person to live with art of high quality. Her art was in her home, not in an institution.

At Sarah Lawrence, I immersed myself again in the theater . . . and married Horace Solomon. I became a day student, and one of three married students in the whole college (it was a rare arrangement in those days). Horace and I moved into an apartment on East 67th Street in the mid-1950s and were faced with the homemaking decisions common to all young couples then. Horace was very clear about his preferences in domestic decor. He loved beautiful eighteenth century American furniture; it was what he had grown up with and what his father collected. Horace also had a treasured collection of posters and drawings by Toulouse-Lautrec which he had purchased in Europe during vacations from Yale. But Horace didn't much care about contemporary art. I remember our first disagreement— it was over china, which he loved and about which I knew or cared very little. He was upset about my lack of concern over which pattern of dinnerware we should choose. So we started married life with Horace's elegant taste and my thirst for understanding and collecting contemporary art. I exercized little control over how that first apartment looked; Horace's mother had hired a decorator who did it up in beige and white and installed the obligatory Parsons table. It was a nifty apartment for a young couple, but my only thoughts about its art came down to my still wanting to buy paintings.

Gradually, as a respite from my efforts to become a professional actress, Stanislavsky school, I found myself visiting museums for inspiration. My sister-in-law, already a dedicated collector of contemporary minimal art, began to take me around to the new galleries starting to proliferate in the city. She introduced me to many dealers. One was Richard Bellamy, the owner of the Green Gallery on West 57th Street, who was to play a crucial role in Horace's and my collecting. We began timidly. Horace still felt that if he couldn't have Impressionist paintings, he wasn't interested in buying art. But I went ahead and acquired a sculptured pot by Dan Flavin and a pin sculpture by Lucas Samaras. I bought them from Dick Bellamy on an installment plan.

We had two boys, John and Tom, and needed to move to a larger apartment (that I still occupy). We had to furnish and decorate it, but how could we afford to when we didn't even have the budget for the American antiques Horace favored. So we had to look at and learn about other styles. We settled on simple Louis XVI furniture—it seemed elegant and practical, and even authentic pieces were then not outrageously expensive. With the help of Jay Dorf, an expert in French period styles, we bought what we needed slowly, trying to pick things of lasting value.

Early in the 1960s, Horace and I were sent by Dick Bellamy to see a happening by Claes Oldenburg. Horace was puzzled that a Yale classmate of his, also an art history major, was orchestrating and participating in such a radical event. My own response to the experience led me to an interest in Andy Warhol's work, and from the Stable Gallery I bought a Warhol Brillo box. When the piece arrived, Horace told the delivery man to put it in the kitchen. Discovering it there, I said, "No, this is a sculpture. I need it as a coffee table in the living room, and let's not discuss whether it's art or furniture." Around this time, Horace read a condemnatory article in a magazine about an artist named Roy Lichtenstein, who was producing paintings about cartoons. For Horace, the work expressed both his childhood and his memories of a popular idiom of American culture—the comic strip. In the article the Leo Castelli gallery was mentioned, and so Horace and I went off and purchased our first Lichtenstein. Little by little, the art we were acquiring became more important than our decor. When I decided to work with another decorator, Richard Hare, I told him, "This apartment must exist in terms of the quality of the art." And that's how he did it. He used pastel colors for the walls and furniture upholstery, and the rooms worked both ways—with art and without a stitch of art. His arrangements were very hospitable, and his decor was not restrictive. The environment was always open to absorb the progress of our collection.

By the mid-1960s, Pop Art was attracting a wider audience as Europeans discovered these works and began to enter the market. When Leon Kraushaar, an American dealer with a vast collection of Pop Art, died, many of his pieces were bought by a man named Stroher, which in turn attracted other German collectors and set prices spiraling upward. By then our whole apartment was filled with Pop Art—Oldenburg, Warhol, James Rosenquist, Lichtenstein, Johns. A Christo storefront had been commissioned for the front hall. The living room was all portraits of women by Warhol and Lichtenstein. The dining room had a Johns, Twombly, Lichtenstein, and Christo, with a table centerpiece by Oldenburg.

We began looking at the work of newer artists. It was the late 1960s, and Richard Bellamy was having shows in conjunction with Noah Godowsky in a gallery on upper Madison Avenue. An exhibition called "Art to Arp" introduced us to the work of Richard Serra and Richard Artschwager. Horace, influenced by Kynaston McShine's still undervalued show, "Information" (Museum of Modern Art, 1969), became deeply intrigued with environmental and minimalist art. We began collecting the next generation of artists, among them Joseph Kosuth, Bruce Nauman, Walter De Maria, Dennis Oppenheim, and Neil Jenney. As became quickly apparent to us, it is almost axiomatic in the world of contemporary art that one artist leads to another. Walter De Maria introduced us to the painter Susan Hall, one of the first artists to deal explicitly with women's issues and styles in her figurative paintings. That was my first exposure to feminist painting and, more important, to contemporary art concerned with a subjectively narrated complex of images. It was a breakthrough for me to see these paintings that represented a fantasy world, an inner life of subjects not usually treated in modern paintings. Other galleries dedicated to showing very experimental artists were also catalysts in our education as collectors. At the Bykert and Dwan galleries we saw the formal conceptual "earth art" of Brice Marden and Walter De Maria, respectively, and the John Gibson gallery featured the experimental pieces of Dennis Oppenheim and work by Italy's Arte Povera group. We came to know the artists, bought their works, and became part of the small but vital scene of "conceptual art." The Whitney Museum produced wonderfully controversial exhibitions that led to vigorous arguments, and the Museum of Modern Art set aside an area, "The Special Projects Room," for avant-garde art. It was all still a small, rather intimate world composed of a few galleries, artists, curators, collectors, and a handful of critics; a world more like an extended family than one characterized by power dealings and large financial transactions.

While Pop Art had contributed to my development as an actress, taking me from the inner understandings of Lee Strasberg's Stanislavky method of acting into perceptions of an outer reality, conceptual and minimalist art propelled me into a new freedom of expression, and I began to write conceptual plays. I also had to accept the realization that my pursuit of an acting career was going no place.

Finding ourselves increasingly immersed in the contemporary art world, Horace and I decided in 1969 to open a space in SoHo devoted to performances, readings, and exhibitions. I saw it as a place where I could produce and direct my conceptual plays, as well as an environment for all the activities of the artists and poets in whom we had come to believe. 98 Greene Street became the venue for virtually every kind of show and performance.

At that time only Paula Cooper and Ivan Karp had opened galleries in SoHo, and it was still an area that seemed frightening and mysterious to many people. Artists, attracted by vast spaces and cheap rents, had moved their studios to the old, vacant loft buildings, but it was very hard to get an audience to come there. For our own place at 98 Greene Street, I asked Gordon Matta-Clark—a young artist with an architectural degree from Cornell whom I represented, and who had his own alternate space at 112 Greene—to design and build it, and the genius of his work was a large factor in our eventual success.

This was the era of social and political upheaval, of Viet Nam and "flower power," Woodstock and the Weatherman Underground. At 98 Greene Street we showed movies by Roger Welsh and Peter Hutchinson; we had poetry readings and put on plays. Artists searching for an alternative to the reductionism of minimalist art were appropriating other mediums and cultures for new sources. They were realizing that aspects of other cultures and of decorative traditions were inspirational material. Neil Jenney assembled paintings in a library-like installation. The painter Brad Davis exhibited paintings of swastikas, returning the symbol to its Indian roots, away from its Fascist connotations. Robert Kushner arranged and performed in his own versions of a fashion show. Thomas Lanigan-Schmidt exhibited a devotional environment with musical background. Kim MacConnel borrowed inspiration from third world cultures in his unframed, unstretched fabric paintings. A strong kind of personal narrative expressionism developed with these artists.

By 1973, more and more galleries had sprung up and established this new art, with increased participation from museums, and we began to feel that 98 Greene Street had served its purpose. It had certainly allowed me to become more intensely involved in the methods and thinking processes of an entire group of artists. Eventually we turned over our equipment to

Right: *"This house was extremely controversial in the Pop Art days,"* says Holly Solomon of this view of the Solomon apartment in its sixties incarnation. *She is seated with her two sons beneath the portrait Roy Lichtenstein painted of her in 1964.*

Below: *Ned Smyth's "Garden" installation dominated the apartment hallway during the late seventies. The changing art in the apartment reflected the evolution in the Solomons' interest from Pop Art to art that incorporated narrative, decorative, and political influences.*

Above: *Never afraid of too much color, Holly Solomon during the late seventies installed Robert Kushner's lushly colored and emphatically patterned fabric painting of women's faces over Kim MacConnel's repainted sofa whose patterns pay homage to Matisse.*

Left: *A tinsel-and-cellophane centerpiece by Thomas Lanigan-Schmidt was juxtaposed with a crystal chandelier and antique Directoire table and chairs in the apartment dining room in happy contravention of conventional decorating rules.*

a new space, The Kitchen, which was to become one of the most important outlets for new music and video. The generative days of 98 Greene Street had come to a close.

In 1973 and 1974, the contemporary art world in New York, reflecting the city's financial crisis and general civic malaise, came to a temporary but traumatic halt. The "correct" word from whatever prominent authority of the time was that "painting is dead." New art wasn't selling. Going against the prevailing gloom, I decided, with Horace's blessing, to open a new gallery in SoHo, at 392 West Broadway, again designed and built by Gordon Matta-Clark, with a loosely related group of young artists engaged in narrative and radically decorative works. Rents were cheap, and I calculated that I could afford to keep a gallery going for three years before making a profit. I felt a strong affinity for these works that no one else wanted to support—the "pattern art" of Kim MacConnel and Robert Kushner, as it came to be known, and the idiosyncratic work of Brad Davis, Laurie Anderson, and Gordon Matta-Clark, among others—and I didn't believe for a moment that painting was dead. These artists were confronting ideas from other cultures, other mediums, dissolving the borders between art and design, art and technology, art and architecture. Everything from ethnic themes to waste recycling to Matisse colors in rugs and textiles was appropriated. It was "new image" work, high culture and low culture in anomalous configuration.

I had my SoHo gallery for seven years. During that time the area became a strange kind of outdoor, culturally congested urban mall for virtually every style of artistic consumption. Our openings grew so crowded that three-quarters of the people would be milling on the street, not even able to get into the gallery!

In 1983, I decided to move uptown. The decision was prompted by SoHo's escalating rents—landlords were getting rentals as high as those on 57th Street—and because of my feeling that a midtown location would encourage a broader and different audience for the art, as well as constitute a challenge for the artists. Some of the artists stayed with me, some did not, and over the years I have taken on others. Through my education as a dealer these past twenty years, through all the changes over that time in cultural and artistic expression, I have been proud and grateful not just for my accomplishments, but even more for the opportunity . . . to have been able to immerse myself in aspects of artistic life I could never have imagined when I dreamed that someday I would have "a real oil painting."

2. A Dealer's View

The great homes I have been privileged to visit are all distinctly personal in their choice of furniture and decor, but the art collections are so superb that they impart to everything a profound radiance that goes beyond the usual sense of "home."

What is collecting, and what constitutes a collector? I've considered these questions many times, and it seems to me that art collectors are unusual people who have refined an ability to think for themselves, and to conceptualize in a curious and independent way. They put things together without thinking in a linear fashion or according to apparently logical patterns and sense of direction. Some seem able to intuit the essence of an artist. Others are attracted to a particular composition which will be repeated in different paintings in subtly different ways. Others are obsessed with gathering a piece of history, a particular moment. Often they cannot explain why they choose one thing over another. I once spent long hours poring over an artist's body of work with a collector who was highly knowledgable about contemporary art. As he went on proclaiming one painting better than the next, I couldn't follow or understand his reasoning. But when I visited his home, a place dominated by red brick walls, I realized that his taste was largely dictated by the color of red brick! His entire collection was built around it, even though he could claim many other reasons for his acquisitions. And everything had quality. Another distinguished collector of superb modern paintings assembles his collection with an underlying attraction to the square. He owns no distinctly horizontal or vertical works, and so I never show him any.

As a dealer in contemporary art, I have discovered the futility of trying to force someone into collecting. I can be encouraging, I can try to teach or to share what I have learned, and I always try to explain or put things in a context so the person can make his or her own decisions. But I can't be so presumptuous as to insist that someone buy a work. Still, if I really believe in a collector—sensing his tastes as reflected in the place where he lives—I will try harder to get him to acquire an important picture. It's a key point: When you live with quality, you begin to absorb its attributes. So when I walk into someone's home and find art of inferior quality on the walls, I don't even try to sell them anything. I'm also wary of the person who comes to me and says, "I'm going to invest in art." With money as your primary motivation, you're almost bound to make mistakes in what you choose.

What always pays in the long run is to *get good advice.* If you needed a doctor, wouldn't you go to the best doctor you could find? When you are learning about art and decor, the same principle applies: Consult the experts. No reputable dealer will try to deceive or short-change you. Dealers are committed to their business, and it would be foolish for their reputations to try to fool you. A good dealer will share his perceptions and allow you to make your own decisions. But then, once a dealer has come to know you, and insists that a work is right for you, take it as a compliment, not a hard sell.

Some collectors are motivated by an historical vision, pursuing their collection as a course of study with a preservationist's urge to isolate a slice of cultural activity. Such collectors work like detectives, tracking down documents, drawings, or texts that illuminate the period which interests them, as well as gathering together significant works of that period. Others enjoy acquiring works that encompass certain schools of painting, certain "movements"; they concentrate on Impressionism, Abstract Expressionism, realism, or new image with an almost encyclopedic fervor. Others search for works that are central to an artist's thought—breakthrough works that demonstrate the artist's highest moment of skill or a significant shift in ideas. Some collectors I have known are magpies, unable to resist objects of varying charm or importance, spurred on always by an insistent, even omniverous need to collect. Still others concentrate on the careers of one or two artists, buying works in all media, and in depth, in order to represent the full range of the artist's creative trajectories. I have heard of one such collector—a passionate, long-time devotee of Mondrian—who had to give up his house and many other possessions during the stringencies of World War II; but he kept all of his Mondrians even when he had no place to hang them. To have sold even one would have been a betrayal of the artist to whom the man had devoted his life. Another contemporary American collector I know always seems to choose the pivotal work of an emerging artist just before that artist secures a reputation with a wider public. On the other hand, there are collectors who always seem to "miss"—they buy the "right" artist but the wrong work; they choose the bargain picture rather than the outstanding picture; or they mistake novelty for originality and quality.

Remember when you collect art that you are selecting objects from an artist's entire body of work—past, present, and future. (This is one reason why it is generally easier, though usually more expensive, to buy older art—that is, after the artist has died and his *oeuvre* is complete.) Most people can understand this autobiographical concept when it comes to books or music, but they find it difficult to apply to the visual arts. What they forget is that art too is history—a shifting, developing accrual of different creative vocabularies that are at once of their time and, the best of them, timeless.

I believe that an artist whose work is significant teaches us about many things around us, and that a great artist involves us not only with his own ideas concerning art but also with the larger issues of our world, including recognition of our own creativity. We learn, and as we learn we in turn may become as passionate and consumed and committed as the artist. There are many successful people who have made fortunes and exercise considerable power in their businesses. They are able to acquire anything they want. Why do they choose to buy art? Not because it reflects power and status, but because it conveys meaning beyond that of a valuable commodity. Art is one of the building blocks of civilization. It teaches and passes on to ensuing generations the bases of creating their own art.

It's easy to assume that collecting requires wealth and sophisticated taste, but in my experience collecting is most fundamentally about growth and discovery. A work of art is a conduit to a certain clarity of vision. Paintings become symbols of understanding, and ultimately they become reminders of the acquisition of that understanding. Sometimes you may acquire a work you don't initially understand, but months or years later it suddenly reveals its meaning to you. Good art has longevity, and in the act of collecting it you document your life.

So in the end, collecting is really cultivating knowledge. Though some people appear to be born with intuitive reasoning, most need to learn. Never be afraid to ask others in order to learn, especially artists. Ally yourself with those who know more than you do. Never be intimidated, and never feel inadequate. Ignorance is not demeaning, and you shouldn't presume to know something when you don't; that's arrogance, and arrogance is self-defeating.

An affinity for something is only a first step. You must next question why you respond to it, and then, depending on the personal satisfaction of that answer, and buttressed by what you have learned, make your decision. It usually doesn't serve to agonize. Another guideline: It's perfectly okay, if you get confused, to allow your *memory* to work for you. Art must be memorable—it must stick in your head after all the data—and in the process of choosing it, you exercise your intelligence to tell you *your* truth. And then, living with *your* art, collecting becomes an enduring way of life. It creates your life story in dimensions physical, emotional, and intellectual. It becomes your legacy to the future.

Opposite top: *The apartment underwent its third transformation during 1987–88. Kim MacConnel's whimsical window treatment for the living room boards up the view but lets in the light. A Warhol soup can painting from the Pop Art days is hung in concert with works by Izhar Patkin (who also created the pink curtains and their red bows as a decorative element for the room) and many of the other artists Holly Solomon now represents in her gallery.*

Opposite bottom: *Another view of the redecorated living room, with its furniture upholstered in three shades of pink, is dominated by a painting by Nicholas Africano and by a Kim MacConnel lamp.*

Above: *Izhar Patkin was commissioned to create a new environmental work for the dining room. His rubber curtain mural, made for all four walls of the room, celebrates food, fruits, and flowers.*

Left: *Holly Solomon's bedroom was redone to incorporate a hutch-cabinet television set as a hybrid of delft china and chinoiserie. Over the set hangs Brad Davis's "Pelican and Water Lilies"; on right wall, "Ballerinas" by Robert Kushner.*

APPENDIX

1. Acquiring Art: Some Practical Advice

Starting out as an art collector can be both intimidating and fascinating. You've looked at works of art enough to have established your areas of interest. You've attended museums and gallery exhibitions, examined permanent collections, and read the magazines, periodicals, and books assiduously enough to have focused your interests. And perhaps you've become familiar enough with the galleries accessible to you to know which of them have works you like. But how do you actually begin buying art?

Working with Dealers

A good art dealer should serve the collector at all stages of his or her development, both as guide and supplier. Our conversations with seasoned collectors again and again revealed the significant influence and inspiration a dedicated and knowledgeable dealer has to offer. Lydia Malbin (Chapter 25) cites her important working relationship with Rose Fried, Pierre Matisse, and Kurt Valentin. California producer and collector Douglas Cramer (Chapter 33) counts several dealers as friends as well as professional colleagues and advisors.

Never be afraid to introduce yourself to a dealer, and don't hesitate to ask questions at the galleries about artists whose work interests you. The gallery owner and staff are there to serve you and to provide you with explanations of their exhibitions and the work of the artists they show. They may also be able to provide you with catalogues and biographies as well as other written materials about their artists. Part of their job is to provide a context of ideas and information for the art they exhibit and sell.

Dealers may work privately—that is, by appointment—or they may run galleries open to the public. Whether private or public, dealers want the art they show to be included in serious collections. They will take pains to share their knowledge and their opinions with collectors they judge to be committed patrons. They will also welcome queries from fledgling collectors eager for information.

Reputable dealers believe in the artists they represent. They have chosen each one from an enormous pool of practicing artists (and estates of deceased artists) because they find merit and vision in a particular body of work. They are gambling on their artists' abilities to develop ideas and techniques over time.

Sometimes the gamble does not pay off, but the best dealers have the ability to find and nurture significant new work that will find its place in art history. Dealers also provide a showcase for older art that has been ratified by time. Often they recommend that the collector concentrate on buying an artist's work in depth. The discriminating collector is the beneficiary of the dealer's hard-won knowledge and artistic discrimination.

Collectors who exclusively look for bargains usually make mistakes. Try to get the finest example rather than the best deal. When buying a work of art from a gallery, you can always ask for the best price. Many galleries provide a 10% "museum" discount to their regular collectors. And they will often allow a collector with good credit to pay for his purchase in installments over six months to a year. Dealers, like everyone else, appreciate courteous clients who reliably and promptly pay their bills. These are the clients who are more likely to get the best service from the gallery.

It's risky to buy art without seeing the actual piece. Collectors should think twice before making a purchase based only on photographs or slides of the work being considered. The object itself will undoubtedly be either superior or inferior to its mechanical reproduction. If the collector cannot actually get to see the work in question, he then must rely on the judgment of the dealer.

Collectors also may wish to ask what a given dealer's policy is on buying back the works of art he has sold. While there are few guarantees, certain galleries and dealers are happy to repurchase items for the original selling price, or even at a higher price reflecting current market value. A gallery may also allow you to exchange one work for another.

While the history of collecting has its share of sensational tales of unscrupulous professionals, most serious dealers are both trustworthy and reputable. Do ascertain a dealer's reputation among his peers. Is he a member of the Art Dealer's Association? This New York-based organization has as its members many of the most established art dealers. Though there are some who consider the ADA restrictively and unnecessarily exclusive, it is a starting place to check up on a gallery's reputation. (Of course many younger, perfectly reputable dealers may not be members.) Also ask curators of local museums, other collectors, even other dealers to recommend dealers to you. Has the gallery or dealer been in business long enough to have dedicated and satisfied clients as well as satisfied artists? Are the artists represented also included in other museum and gallery shows, and in other serious collections? Does the gallery have a reputation for good business practices? There are questions the collector should ask in his search for the art he desires.

Buying at Auction

The expansion of the auction market during the last fifteen years has had a profound impact on the buying and selling of art. The increasingly global reach of multi-national auction houses like Sotheby's and Christie's has attracted buyers from all over the world, pushing up prices and increasing competition for desired works of all kinds, from modern and contemporary art to old masters, and from antique furniture to free-form twentieth-century design. It is no longer uncommon for auction houses in New York or Chicago to conduct many of their sales with telephone bidders calling from the far ends of the earth. Once mainly the province of dealers—a true wholesale market—the art auction is now an arena where collector, dealers, and museums compete in the bidding—a true retail market. Auctions may be the place for the informed collector to find a specific work he wishes to add to his collection or to spot an undervalued item.

Buying at auction can be dangerous for the uninformed or the impulsive. Auction fever is by now a well-documented phenomenon and buyers need to remember that while the auction is a genuine marketplace, it is also a theater where bidders can get carried away and where prices sometimes may be skillfully manipulated.

If you do see a piece you desire coming up for auction, check the estimated price listed by the auction house and determine also whether there is a reserve price, the price below which the item will not be sold. Some auctions are conducted without reserve limits. It's also wise to find out recent prices for comparable pieces by checking with galleries on roughly equivalent works. If it's an older work and no equivalent gallery prices are readily available, consult the annually published auction price indexes.

You should also research the provenance and condition of the work under consideration. A gallery representing the artist who made the piece can help you establish its previous owners and whereabouts if they are not clearly indicated in the auction catalogue. If you are unsure whether the object has been repaired, cleaned, or restored, you may wish to enlist a qualified conservator to examine it for you. Getting a conservator's opinion, especially if the item is going to be expensive, is well worth a reputable conservator's fee.

Some collectors appoint dealers or other agents to bid for them at auction. This method of buying is common when a well-known collector can't be present or wants to remain anonymous. It's also a way of not paying too much, since the appointed bidder cannot go beyond the price designated by the collector.

Art Fairs

The art fair, once a more common event in Europe than in the United States, is becoming a fixture on the American art scene. Now there are fairs worldwide, with one planned for nearly every month in the year. New York, Madrid, Paris, Cologne, Hamburg, Los Angeles, and Chicago all are host cities to regularly scheduled fairs. While the fairs held in Basel, Switzerland, and, more recently, in Madrid, Spain, as well as the beleaguered Venice Biennale, provide an approximate overview of current European and some American art, the Chicago Art Fair, held annually in May at Chicago's vast Navy Pier, has become a major American nexus of varied displays from dozens of American and a few European art dealers, providing collectors with an exciting opportunity to see an enormous range and selection of modern and contemporary art. Many collectors who are unable to travel frequently to New York or Europe find that spending several days at such fascinating—if exhausting—art events a good way to hone their powers of selectivity. Fairs are also a fine place to discover artists whose work is regional or not yet widely known.

Increasingly people choose to buy art at such fairs, or to make contact with unfamiliar dealers and galleries who may later be called or seen about the works they showed. Regional or private dealers who might otherwise be inaccessible regularly participate at art fairs. Antiques shows can also be useful places to look at a wide variety of art and objects. And smaller fairs around the country, while they may not demonstrate the quality or breadth of selection found in Chicago, also can be useful hunting grounds for collectors.

At first, any art fair (or antiques show) is confusing if not overwhelming, but a preliminary walk-through will reveal what is interesting and what stands out from the endless atmosphere of sameness that may at first seem to prevail. Make notes. Then, after your initial survey, you'll have a memory aid to direct your return to specific works. And if you are hesitant about buying on the spot, you can always contact the dealer or gallery later.

The Artist's Studio

Buying directly from an artist is an experience that tests the collector's powers of judgment, not to mention his manners. If the artist is not represented by a gallery, the studio is probably the only place to see a wide selection of his current and past efforts. But even if an artist is represented by a gallery, the collector may still want to arrange a studio visit to become more familiar with how the painter or sculptor works. Since such a visit is also a social situation, it's important to be courteous, whether or not you make a purchase. When buying directly from an artist who is also represented by a dealer, remember that you are expected to pay a gallery commission even though you may not have gone through the dealer.

Other Sources

Some collectors have found interesting things at museum shops or through sale exhibitions which museums often hold. And there are other, sometimes overlooked sources, such as museum or other charity auctions of art where a part or all of the price can become a charitable tax deduction. Even yard sales can yield interesting art.

Whether you end up buying from a gallery, an auction, an art fair, a museum show, or from the artist himself, remember that the real object is to acquire something that has meaning to you. The idea of buying art as an investment is and always has been misguiding as a *primary* reason to collect. Though historically important art will probably increase in monetary value, other investments are far less risky for making a quick profit. What you gain from owning a work of art goes far beyond such considerations. It comes down to a matter of inner commitment, and the many kinds of satisfaction to be gained from possessing something you love.

2. Conservation Considerations

All works of art are subject to the erosive effects of time and to destructive accidents. But modern paintings and drawings have become a particular nightmare for art conservators (and for collectors). Many modern masterpieces are crumbling, the result of what restorers call "inherent vice." This term refers to the fact that certain works of art contain the seeds of their own decay. In scores of cases, the new materials and experimental methods used by so many modern and contemporary painters have contravened the rules of chemistry and stable materials that have constituted traditional techniques of painting. In the words of a Manhattan conservator, "Contemporary paintings are rarely built to last."

"In their later years, many artists are witnessing the effects of their spontaneity," said Denise Domergue, the Museum of Modern Art's trained conservator, in a recent magazine interview. "They watch their earlier work crack, cleave, and in some cases just fall apart. The changes in some works are quite drastic." Works painted by Franz Kline on newsprint are notoriously fragile, as the acid-loaded paper discolors and actually crumbles.

The translucent washes of Mark Rothko's delicate color surfaces are tending to turn to powder and fading, while the works of Color Field painters like Morris Louis and Helen Frankenthaler, painted with radically thinned colors on unprimed cotton duck, cannot really be cleaned without washing away a layer of color. "These pictures should really be treated like tapestries," says New York painting conservator Hallie Halpern. "They, like any work painted on unprimed canvas, are extremely subject to irreversible discoloration and a weakening of the canvas fibers. Fingerprints are almost impossible to remove from unprimed canvas." Shoddy stretchers warp, and materials like felt and velvet have a short half-life. Julian Schnabel's encrusted plate paintings are notorious in conservation circles; plates fall off with distressing regularity. Anselm Kiefer's canvases are as fragile as his allegories are profound. His extensive use of straw, poured lead, even dried ferns mean serious restoration problems for the owner in the near as well as the more distant future. One conservator has advised, "If you want to have an Anselm Kiefer in 25 years, buy it and put it horizontally under glass. You'll have the only one left. Never before has the work of an artist of high value and high interest been so self-destructive."

If, as Hallie Halpern warns, "many contemporary paintings are time bombs waiting to explode," what is the collector to do? Given the fragility of works of art, it is surprising how few collectors really consider potential conservation problems when caught in the excitement of buying art.

An awareness of potential risk is a first step. Another precaution the collector might take—especially when considering an older work that may already have been subject to cleaning and restoration—is to have a reputable conservator examine the picture at the gallery or auction house. This is one way to tell if poorly done conservation has damaged or diminished the work. Relining, cleaning, extensive patching, or the faulty inpainting of cracks can all be detrimental to a painting. In certain cases, restoration may have been so extensive that virtually none of the original picture is left. Halpern also advises that "the less work you do on a picture, the better." Many restorers spend a major portion of their time trying to repair the ravages of previous restoration jobs.

When buying a work by a living artist, the collector might even ask the artist about it. What are his technical methods? Is he trying to make lasting works or does he not care about longevity? While risk and experimentation may be concomitants of the daring artist, the collector has every right to pause when faced with fugitive or fragile materials and untested painting techniques. Since it is hardly to the advantage of dealers and others who sell contemporary art works to bring up possible conservation problems, the collector himself must be aware of potential pitfalls. It is your decision whether or not you wish to spend a substantial amount of money on a fragile or damaged work, and it is your responsibility to know what repairs are and are not feasible. Remember that in certain cases, the work might not be salvageable. In others, as with antique furniture, restoration may diminish the market value of the work.

Even the most well-crafted artworks can deteriorate when attacked by light and humidity. The most dangerous time for any work is when it is being moved. Then, especially, it may be dropped, punctured, or cracked. Paintings should not be hung over radiators or close to doors where a doorknob might smash into the surface, or where there are constant drafts of warm or cold air. Extreme changes in temperature and humidity cause paper and canvas to ''exercise''—that is, to expand and contract—and repeated exercise weakens the fibers and can cause paints to crack and pastels and charcoals to flake. If an art work goes out on loan to an exhibition, its condition should be carefully checked before and after the event.

When damage does occur, or when a picture or sculpture does need restoration, what should a collector know about getting the proper help? Many experts warn against using a restorer who is also a dealer or an appraiser, given the possible conflicts of interest. To find a reputable conservator, experts recommend consulting the conservation department of a respected museum. Research any potential restorer from their list as thoroughly as possible. Or one can seek help from studio workshops. The small ones usually can oversee an entire restoration process, while larger studios tend to work on an assembly-line basis. However, very large canvases may well require a bigger studio. ''A very large picture is a conservator's potential headache,'' says one restorer.

Restorers charge more for work on a very valuable picture because of hefty insurance premiums, and they may also charge more for work on contemporary pictures because of their experimental materials and techniques. You should always ask the restorer for a written estimate, one that includes not only the cost of the job but also the time the conservator thinks it will take. Then ask the conservator to call you if costs should deviate substantially from the original estimate. Typical conservation costs range from a few hundred to several thousands of dollars, so in some cases it may be preferable to live with the results of age and time and do nothing to the art. Besides, there are problems that restoration cannot always repair, and after a certain point conservation would entail the complete reconstruction of the work. On the other hand, one shouldn't avoid conservation when it can substantially add to the life of a work. Mending cracks and rips is usually not expensive and is well worth the trouble. Any such damage should, in fact, be repaired as soon as possible, since it can only get worse with time. Finally, every completed conservation job should also come with a written conservation report detailing the restorer's work.

Conservators are specialists. Someone who restores paintings will not generally work on drawings or works on paper. Sculpture, photography, textiles, ceramics, furniture, metal objects, all present distinct problems that require the correct expert knowledge. Procedures are often controversial. In the field of photography, for example, the process known as enhancement is frowned upon by most conservators. It is a process which can restore a very faded black and white photograph to pristine clarity and contrast. But it is irreversible, and conservation ethics *demand* that procedures must be reversible. Collectors must be aware of such controversies and of the safety of proposed procedures. Those who are forewarned, especially in today's expanded and exploding art market, can avoid buying damaged or dangerously deteriorating works. Or, if you must have that Kiefer, you will at least be aware of the fugitive nature of your investment.

3. Art Insurance, Collection Documentation, and other Security Matters

Issues of insurance and security are often an overlooked aspect of art collecting. While most people insure their homes and the contents of those homes under standard policies as a matter of course, a collector of art and other valuable furniture or objects faces a more complex insurance situation. Some collectors do not take out separate art insurance policies because they fear that a dishonest insurance broker or insurance company employee might subsequently target their collections for theft; others feel that the insurance fees will be onerously expensive or simply don't get around to the appraisals and paperwork such policies entail.

Actually, fine art insurance (excluding jewelry) is one of the least expensive forms of insurance available. In New York City, rates run anywhere from 14 cents to 19 cents per $100 of value annually, an excellent rate compared to what insuring a boat or a house costs.

There are companies who insure art exclusively. These firms usually work in conjunction with other insurance firms that provide general homeowner's coverage. Huntington Block, Hoag Robinson, and, to a lesser extent, Marsh & McLennan, are all firms that specialize in art insurance policies. Because the values of art works and antiques have risen so sharply over the past twenty years, insurance has become all the more crucial for the serious collector.

Try to find a firm whose brokers appreciate the nature of the collection, and ask whether it employs a full-time art-and-furniture expert (many brokers are completely unfamiliar with artistic material). Since the product offered is similar regardless of the firm, what collectors must demand from any company they select is *service*. A good insurance broker will shop for the best insurance arrangement for his client and can act as intermediary between the client and the insurance company, whereas an insurance agent is the representative of only one company.

The broker or insurance agent you select should offer certain services beyond the basic ones. As well as looking for the best rates and the most comprehensive services, he should assist you in cataloguing, visually documenting, and periodically updating the inventory of your collection. He should be able to provide a list of reputable appraisers or appraisal companies, and the companies in turn should assure you of a speedy and courteous settlement of any claims for theft, loss, or damage. Any evasiveness by the broker or agent about this issue is a reason to go elsewhere. It is also advisable to decide between your agent or broker and your insurance company who the insurance adjuster will be should a substantial loss occur.

To insure your collection, you will need to have its value appraised. The Appraisers' Association of America can provide a list of licensed appraisers specializing in different fields. Another organization, The Art Dealers' Association of America, also appraises individual works of art, charging a fee based on a percentage of the appraised value of the piece. While the major auction houses often have appraisal departments, their primary interest is in acquiring material to auction off rather than in services, and since the appraisal branch of an auction house can be a convenient opportunity to scout out potential sales material, there may be a conflict of interest. An independent appraiser is likely to be more disinterested. While people like to have insurance appraisals that are high, they also want estate appraisals that are low. Thus insurance appraisals tend to be higher than estate appraisals. The logic here is that the cost of replacing an object will be more than what was paid for it orig-

inally, while tax considerations make a low estate appraisal desirable.

People often choose not to insure their art to avoid the inclusion of a document for the IRS in their estate. In many such cases the families pass on furniture and art works informally, essentially keeping them beyond the purview of the taxable estate. The disadvantage of this practice is that there is no reimbursement if something is lost, destroyed, or stolen. Of course one can put aside a certain sum of money as "self-insurance," essentially saving the premium money one would have paid to an insurance company and assuring one's privacy as well.

An updated inventory of the objects in your collection is vital to have whether or not it is used for insurance purposes. Sometimes a general appraisal of everything is adequate; in other cases, specialists should be consulted. A written inventory is only a beginning. Insurance companies strongly recommend that each object in the collection be photographed and that all relevant data such as medium, size, height, artist, and provenance be recorded. A more recent technique for making a record is to create a videotape of the objects and paintings. It should focus on individual, valuable items. If you do have a policy—even a floater policy that is attached to your basic homeowner's insurance—list the number of the object as recorded in that policy and write pertinent information on a card to be placed next to the object when you make the videotape or photograph. This can facilitate identification if a claim is made.

Don't keep your visual record and your insurance policy at home. In the event of fire, this could mean that your documentation would disappear along with objects from your collection. Put the documentation in a safe located elsewhere, not in some house repository.

When you do take out insurance, the insurance company will demand that you have an adequate security system and will lay out security guidelines. Sometimes collectors have installed these systems to comply with insurance company demands only to hardly ever turn them on. Though a good electronic security system may be expensive, it is an important safeguard for the serious collection.

4. A Directory of Recommended Art Services and Sources

APPRAISALS

Appraisers Association of America
60 East 42 Street
New York, New York 10165

Art Dealers Association of America
575 Madison Avenue
New York, New York 10022

Art Dealers Association of California
718 North La Cienega Boulevard
Los Angeles, California 90069

Kelvyn G. Lilley
666 Lake Shore Drive
Chicago, Illinois 60610

ART HANDLERS

Contemporary Installations
5769 West Venice Boulevard
Los Angeles, California 90019

L.A. Packing & Crating
8501 Steller Drive
Culver City, California 90230

Icon Services
764 North Milwaukee Avenue
Chicago, Illinois 60622

Judson Art Warehouse
49-20 Fifth Street
Long Island, New York 11101

Lebron Brothers
31-36 58th Street
Woodside, New York 11377

INSURANCE

Chubb & Sons, Inc.
100 Williams Street
New York, New York 10005

Huntington T. Block Insurance
2101 L Street N.W.
Washington, D.C. 20037

Marsh & McLennan, Inc.
1221 Avenue of the Americas
New York, New York 10020

ART LENDING SERVICES

Art Rental Gallery
L. A. County Museum of Art
5905 Wilshire Boulevard
Los Angeles, California 90036

Art Rental and Sales Gallery
The Art Institute of Chicago
Michigan Avenue at Adams
Chicago, Illinois 60603

Art Rental and Sales Gallery
Cedar Rapids Museum of Art
324 Third Street, S.E.
Cedar Rapids, Iowa

The Sales & Rental Gallery
The Detroit Institute of the Arts
5200 Woodward Avenue
Detroit, Michigan 48202

Members Gallery
The Albright Knox Art Gallery
1285 Elmwood Avenue
Buffalo, New York, 14222

Rental Sales Gallery
The Portland Art Museum
1219 S.W. Park Avenue
Portland, Oregon 97205

Art Sales & Rental Gallery
The Philadelphia Museum of Art
26 Street and The Benjamin
   Franklin Parkway
Philadelphia, Pennsylvania 19101

AUCTION HOUSES

Christie's
342 North Rodeo Drive
Beverly Hills, California 90210

Christie's
200 West Superior Street
Chicago, Illinois 60610

Christie's
502 Park Avenue
New York, New York 10021

Doyle
178 East 87 Street
New York, New York 10028

Leslie Hindman Auctioneers
215 West Ohio
Chicago, Illinois 60610

Phillips
406 East 79 Street
New York, New York 10021

Sotheby's
308 North Rodeo Drive
Beverly Hills, California 90210

Sotheby's
840 North Michigan Avenue
Chicago, Illinois 60610

Sotheby's
1334 York Avenue
New York, New York 10021

BOOKSTORES AND CATALOGUES

Art & Architecture Books
5514 Wilshire Boulevard
Los Angeles, California 90036

Art Catalogues
625 North Almont Drive
Los Angeles, California 90069

Metropolis Books
634 North Robertson Boulevard
Los Angeles, California 90048

Hacker Art Books
54 West 57 Street
New York, New York 10019

Jaap Rietman, Inc.
134 Spring Street
New York, New York 10012

Ursus Books
39 East 78 Street
New York, New York 10021

Weyhe Art Books
794 Lexington Avenue
New York, N.Y. 10021

Wittenborn Art Books
1018 Madison Avenue
New York, New York 10021

CONSERVATION

The American Institute for
   Conservation of Historic
   and Artistic Works
3545 Williamsburg Lane
N.W. Washington, D.C. 20008

Professional Picture
   Framers Association
P.O. Box 7655
Richmond, Virginia 23231

STOLEN ART

The International Foundation
   for Art Research, Inc.
New York, N.Y. 10021
IFAR provides reports on stolen art,
antiques, porcelain, and furniture
in reports issued ten times a year.
The organization maintains an
archive of reported thefts that is
open to queries. File search fee is
$25.